EYEWITNESS TRAVEL

TOP 10
NEW ENGLAND

W9-BLE-703

PATRICIA HARRIS
& DAVID LYON

Penguin
Random
House

Top 10 New England Highlights

The Top 10 of Everything

CONTENTS

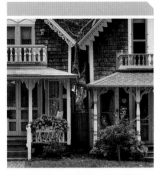

New England Area by Area

Streetsmart

Within each Top 10 list in this book, no hierarchy of quality or popularity is implied. All 10 are, in the editor's opinion, of roughly equal merit.

Throughout this book, floors are referred to in accordance with American usage; i.e., the "first floor" is at ground level.

Front cover and spine *Stunning fall colors and lakefront house, Highland Lake, New Hampshire*
Back cover *Picturesque Portland Head, Maine's oldest Lighthouse*
Title page *Colorful display of lobster buoys at Cape Cod, Massachusetts*

Welcome to
New England

From tall ships and lobster boats to hip city bars, from mountain trails and ski runs to leading art museums, from fall foliage to endless summer beaches, New England packs nature, history, and cutting-edge culture into a single compact, drivable region. With Eyewitness Top 10 New England, it's yours to explore.

New England is admired for its oceanfront that ranges from the rockbound coast of Maine, with its endless inlets and spruce-tufted islands, to the sandy beaches of **Cape Cod National Seashore**. In Massachusetts, find the Boston Symphony on the summer lawns of **Tanglewood** in the **Berkshires**. In Connecticut, explore the historic vessels of **Mystic Seaport** and the waterfall-dotted **Litchfield Hills**. Cruise aboard an America's Cup yacht or marvel at the Gilded Age mansions in **Newport**, Rhode Island. The **Green Mountains** of Vermont and the **White Mountains** of New Hampshire glow with colors in the fall, entice through the summer with rivers for rafting and canoeing, and feature some of America's best skiing in winter.

History lives in the countryside around Boston, and factory outlet centers in every state sing their siren song to shoppers. Colorful and tasty festivals abound, from the **Maine Lobster Festival** to Boston's **Independence Day** concert and fireworks.

Whether you're coming for a week or a month, our Top 10 guide brings together the best of everything the region offers, from the pristine woods and shores of **Mount Desert Island** to the chic and sophisticated bars and restaurants of **Boston**. There are tips throughout, from seeking out what's free to avoiding the crowds, plus eight easy-to-follow itineraries, designed to help you catch the highlights of each state in a short span of time. Add inspiring photography and detailed maps, and you have the essential pocket-sized travel companion. **Enjoy the book, and enjoy New England.**

Clockwise from top: **Acadia National Park (Maine)**; *Friendship of Salem*, **Salem Maritime National Historic Site (Massachusetts)**; **Martha's Vineyard (Massachusetts)**; **Block Island (Rhode Island)**; **Boston Freedom Trail symbol**; **Lake Waramaug (Connecticut)**; **Sunday River (Maine)**

Exploring New England

New England packs extremes into a small area – from mountain wilderness to beaches that reach the horizon, from picturesque villages to pulsing cities. Start with two days on foot seeing the historic sights of Boston, then pack the car and head out to explore the rest of New England over the next seven days.

afternoon, spend some time exploring the historic village of **Stockbridge** (see p33) in the **Berkshires** (see pp32–3) and visit the hip town of **Great Barrington** (see p33). For the evening, buy advance tickets for the Boston Symphony (summer only) at **Tanglewood Music Center** (see p33).

Two Days in Boston

Day ❶
MORNING
Take a free Boston Park Ranger walking tour of the first half of the **Freedom Trail** (see p13), from Faneuil Hall to the Old South Meeting House.
AFTERNOON
Join the other free ranger-led Freedom Trail tour from Faneuil Hall to the Old North Church.

Day ❷
MORNING
Start your day with Impressionism and more at Boston's **Museum of Fine Arts** (see p40).
AFTERNOON
Peruse the bookstores of **Harvard Square** (see p69), then see the **Harvard Museum of Natural History** (see p43). At the waterfront, visit the **New England Aquarium** (see p63).

Seven Days in New England

Day ❶
Tour scenic **Lake Waramaug** (see p24) in the **Litchfield Hills** (see p24–5), and climb the trail to the top of **Kent Falls** (see p24). Later in the

Day ❷
In the **Green Mountains** (pp 26–7), visit **Manchester's** (see p27) outlet stores and enjoy the breathtaking views from the **Mount Equinox Skyline Drive** (see p27). Tour **Hildene** (see p26), then drive to the stunning **Lakes Region** (see pp30–31) in New Hampshire.

Day ❸
At the resort of **Weirs Beach** (see p30), explore **Lake Winnipesaukee** (see p30) on board the M/S *Mount Washington* (see p30). Then drive north to Lincoln to follow the **Kancamagus Highway** (see p20) east, stopping for a hike to one of the many waterfalls. Continue east to **Portland** (see pp28–9).

Day ❹
Take a stroll around Portland's **Old Port District** (see p28) and enjoy a seafood lunch. Afterwards, drive to

Lake Winnipesaukee is New Hampshire's largest lake at approximately 21 miles (34 km) long.

Key
— Two-day itinerary
— Seven-day itinerary

Boston's Faneuil Hall has served as a meeting hall and market since 1742.

the magical **Mount Desert Island** (see pp14–15) and visit the lively resort town of **Bar Harbor** (see p14) and the **Abbe Museum** (see p15).

Day ❺

Start the day by exploring the natural wonders of **Cadillac Mountain, Sand Beach,** and **Thunder Hole** (see p15) at Acadia National Park. Lunch early on the lawns at Jordan Pond House (see p14). Then drive south to **Cape Cod** (see pp16–17), stopping to visit the pretty town of **Falmouth** (see p17).

Day ❻

Take a break to relax on the stunning beaches of the **Cape Cod National Seashore** (see p16). In the late afternoon, head down to colorful **Provincetown** (see p17) to enjoy its carnival atmosphere and, later, a fine-dining al fresco meal.

Day ❼

Rent a bike to explore the **Cape Cod Rail Trail** (see p17) and **Nickerson State Park** (see p16). In **Newport** (see pp18–19), marvel at the sumptuous Gilded Age mansion **The Breakers** (see p18). Then admire Newport Harbor on an **America's Cup Charters** cruise (see p18).

Top 10 New England Highlights

Stowe Community Church nestled in
the Green Mountains, Vermont

TOP10 New England Highlights

New England is an all-season destination of pine-scented mountains, ocean villages, urban centers – and so much more. It's also the birthplace of America, a fact attested by historic homes and museums. For many, the region is white churches, covered bridges, snowy ski slopes, blazing fall foliage, lighthouses on craggy cliffs, and lobsters fresh from the sea.

1 Historic Boston
The American past is palpable in New England's largest city, where cobbled streets echo with the calls of patriots and cafés enliven the old Quincy Market *(see pp12–13)*.

2 Mount Desert Island, Maine
Rugged headlands above a crashing ocean, hiking trails crisscrossing pine forests, and still ponds reflecting the sky's blue bowl express nature in all its unbounded wildness *(see pp14–15)*.

3 Cape Cod, Massachusetts
The bent arm of Cape Cod is a world of untamed dunes, bird-filled marshes, and quirky towns where visitors can savor fresh fish and sticky taffy *(see pp16–17)*.

4 Newport, Rhode Island
Opulent mansions on seaside cliffs reveal the splendors of the Gilded Age in this storied yachting harbor *(see pp18–19)*.

Map labels:
Fort Ke
Mountains
Moosehead Lake
Greenvill
MAINE
Appalachian
Rangeley
Augusta
Lake Champlain
VERMONT
Montpelier
White Mountains
Lewiston
Burlington
Green Mountains
Lakes Region
Brunsw
Hanover
Portland
NEW HAMPSHIRE
Concord
Kennebun
Manchester
Portsmouth
Williamstown
Brattleboro
Pittsfield
MASSACHUSETTS
Boston
Springfield
Worcester
Provinceto
Berkshires
Providence
Plymouth
Litchfield Hills
Hartford
RHODE ISLAND
Falmouth
Ca
Co
CONNECTICUT
Mystic
Newport
New Haven

⑤ White Mountains, New Hampshire

Summer hikers and winter skiers relish these rugged, forested mountains. Hike, drive, or ride the cog railway up Mount Washington *(see pp20–21)*.

Presque
Isle

oulton

Lincoln   Calais
angor   Machias
Ellsworth

② Mount
Desert Island

0 km   50
0 miles   50

⑥ Litchfield Hills, Connecticut

Bistros and boutiques fill the white clapboard buildings of hill-country villages in this area where the rich keep country retreats *(see pp24–5)*.

⑦ Green Mountains, Vermont

From pre-Revolutionary villages to ridgeline hiking trails, the Green Mountains form the spine of Vermont. In fall, its forests blaze with color; in winter, some of the nation's top slopes lure skiers *(see pp26–7)*.

⑧ Portland and Casco Bay, Maine

Portland remains a seafaring center on a picturesque bay, but the Old Port also hosts galleries, inns, and boutiques *(see pp28–9)*.

⑨ Lakes Region, New Hampshire

Lake Winnipesaukee, with its 240-mile (386-km) shoreline, rules the region's kingdom of mountain-rimmed lakes *(see pp30–31)*.

⑩ Berkshires, Massachusetts

Theater, music, and dance flourish in the gentle Berkshire Hills, where lavish estates of a bygone era's millionaires lend a sophisticated air to homespun country villages *(see pp32–3)*.

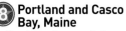

🔟 ⭐ Historic Boston

Founded in 1630 by Puritans who envisioned their settlement as a shining beacon to the world, Boston was among America's first great urban centers. Its patriots led the rebellion that grew into the American Revolution, and few places in the US evoke so vividly the birth of a nation. Centuries later, Boston remains at the national forefront in politics, the arts, culture, education, and science. It retains its Classical proportions, with modern buildings nudging up against landmarks of the Colonial and Revolutionary eras.

1 Massachusetts State House
Completed in 1798, this legislative temple with its ornate marble and paneled halls was architect Charles Bulfinch's masterpiece, and the model for capitols around the country (below).

Map of Historic Boston

3 Black History Trail
Boston's free African American community helped lead the nation in struggles to abolish slavery and achieve equal rights. The trail ends at the African Meeting House.

5 Granary Burying Grounds
Some of Boston's most famous characters are buried at this Tremont Street graveyard of more than 2,300 slate tombstones in the shadow of downtown skyscrapers.

4 Boston Common and Public Garden
Concerts and Shakespeare plays enliven the Common, Boston's green heart since 1634. Tens of thousands of flowers bloom in the Public Garden, while Swan Boats glide on its pond (below).

2 Fenway Park
All baseball fans long to see a game in Fenway. Opened in 1912, this is the oldest Major League Baseball park, and a shrine to the game.

6 Faneuil Hall

One of Boston's most significant Revolutionary sites, Faneuil Hall heard firebrands like Samuel Adams call the populace to open revolt against the king. Public debates are still staged here among the historical portraits in the Great Hall.

9 Old North Church

The spare decor typical of a Colonial house of worship barely hints at the fame of Christ Church **(above)**, where lanterns hung in its belfry signaled British troop movements.

THIS WAY TO HISTORY

The Freedom Trail (a red line on the sidewalk, either paint or bricks) snakes through Boston highlighting important sites of Colonial and Revolutionary history. The 2.5-mile (4-km) walking trail begins at Boston Common and ends with climbing Bunker Hill Monument in Charlestown. Pick up a map and inquire about free, ranger-led Freedom Trail tours at the Boston National Historical Park visitor center at Faneuil Hall (www.nps.gov/bost).

10 Harvard Yard

Free student-led tours through Harvard Yard **(below)** provide an insight into life at America's first and most prestigious university, founded in 1636.

7 Paul Revere House

Revere's house, built around 1680, is the oldest in Boston. During a visit here you get an intimate look at the domestic life of this key figure in the history of the American Revolution.

8 USS Constitution

Now in dry dock, USS *Constitution* is the world's oldest commissioned warship. The three-masted frigate, nick-named "Old Ironsides," has served in the US Navy since 1797, battling North African pirates and foreign navies alike.

NEED TO KNOW

Massachusetts State House: MAP W3; 24 Beacon St

Fenway Park: MAP S5; 4 Yawkey Way

African Meeting House: MAP V3; 46 Joy St

Boston Common and Public Garden: MAP V4

Granary Burying Grounds: MAP W3

Faneuil Hall: MAP X3; Dock Sq

Paul Revere House: MAP X3; 19 North Sq

USS Constitution: MAP W1; Charlestown Navy Yard, 1 Constitution Rd, Charlestown

Old North Church: MAP X2; 193 Salem St

Harvard Yard: MAP S1

■ As you might expect, security is tight at the USS *Constitution*. Don't carry anything you couldn't take on an airplane.

■ Quincy Market food court, adjacent to Faneuil Hall, offers good variety and value for a quick lunch.

TOP 10 ⭐ Mount Desert Island, Maine

Mount Desert Island condenses the fabled Maine coast and woods into a single magical spot. Salt-splashed fishing villages dot the southwest lobe, while Bar Harbor on the east bustles with lodging options and restaurants. Painters of the 19th-century Hudson River School were among the first to celebrate Mount Desert's wild natural beauty, and their art encouraged wealthy industrialists to build summer estates thoughtfully incorporated into natural settings. Half the island falls within Acadia National Park.

1 Jordan Pond House

For a touch of gentility in the wilderness, nothing beats sitting in Adirondack chairs on the grassy lawn of the Jordan Pond House, where you can enjoy their famous popovers with afternoon tea.

2 Carriage Roads

To preserve auto-free tranquility, John D. Rockefeller Jr. built 45 miles (72 km) of carriage roads through land he gave to Acadia National Park – still reserved for hikers, cyclists, skiers, and equestrians.

3 Bar Harbor

Grand mansions line the shore of this lively resort town on Frenchman Bay. Bar Harbor **(above)** functions as a tourist center for the island. It's also a convenient base for visiting Acadia National Park.

4 Bass Harbor Head

At the southern tip of Mount Desert, Bass Harbor Head **(below)** towers above the sea. The lighthouse offers amazing views over the deep blue ocean.

NEED TO KNOW

MAP R3

Acadia National Park Visitor Center: off Rte 3, Hulls Cove; 207 288 3338, 877 444 6777 (camping reservations); open Apr–mid-Jun & Sep–Oct: 8:30am–4:30pm daily; mid-Jun–Aug: 8am–6pm daily; adm; www.nps.gov/acad

Jordan Pond House: Park Loop Rd, Seal Harbor; 207 276 3316; open mid-May–late Oct: 11am–9pm; www.acadiajordanpond house.com

Abbe Museum: 26 Mount Desert St, Bar Harbor; 207 288 3519; open May–Oct: 10am–5pm daily; Nov–Apr: 10am–4pm Thu–Sat; adm; www.abbemuseum.org

■ Acadia National Park is one of the most visited parks in the National Park system. For summer visits, reserve lodgings well in advance.

■ Check out Trenton Bridge Lobster Pound (see p128).

Map of Mount Desert Island

⑤ Cadillac Mountain
It's worth rising early to hike or drive up 1,527-ft (465-m) Cadillac Mountain **(above)** to catch the first rays of the sun to strike the US.

⑥ Thunder Hole
Swift tides and strong waves pounding the craggy ledges at Thunder Hole force air and water into a deep crease beneath the rock. Under the right conditions, a ground-shaking thunderclap echoes from the hole.

⑧ Abbe Museum
Explore 10,000 years of Native-American culture in this museum devoted to the heritage of Maine's Wabanaki peoples. See basketry **(left)** and wood-carving at the small outpost in the National Park in summer.

⑩ Sand Beach
Rugged cliffs and jumbled ledges line most of Acadia's shoreline, but thousands of visitors flock to this 870-ft (265-m) stretch of sandy cove **(below)** to sunbathe. Swimming is bracing, as the ocean water rarely exceeds 55° F (15° C).

⑦ Southwest Harbor
This snug harbor, tucked inside two lobes of Mount Desert Island, is delightfully tranquil and picturesque. Take a lobster-hauling boat ride or catch the Cranberry Isles ferry here.

⑨ Hiking Trails
To penetrate the deep wilderness or get up close and personal with the mountains of Acadia National Park, use the network of more than 120 miles (193 km) of trails. They range from easy to very strenuous.

Cape Cod, Massachusetts

TOP 10 ⭐

Race Point at the tip of Cape Cod feels like the end of the earth. Beyond this long, thin crook of glacial sand lies the broad Atlantic, stretching all the way to Portugal. The Cape's fishing fleets haul the sweetest scallops and richest tuna; virtually every cove harbors a hamlet founded by farmers whose grandchildren turned to the sea. Great Beach extends for 30 miles (48 km), from Chatham to Provincetown, comfortably accommodating the thousands of swimmers and sunbathers who flock here during the summer.

1 **Sandwich Boardwalk and Town Beach**

Songbirds whistle as you walk the Sandwich Boardwalk over Great Marsh. The gentle waves and warm waters at Town Beach make it ideal for children.

2 **Hyannis**
Thanks to its airport and two ferry lines to Nantucket and Martha's Vineyard, Hyannis is Cape Cod's market town and transportation hub.

3 **Cape Cod Canal**
Dug to save ships from the perilous Nantucket Shoals, the canal marks the Cape's sedate beginning **(below)**. Bike down its paths or fish for bass and ferocious bluefish.

4 **Cape Cod National Seashore Beaches**
Beaches for swimmers, kite-flyers, surfers, and sunbathers stretch from Nauset Beach to Race Point, with its historic Life-Saving Station **(above)**.

5 **Nickerson State Park**
Clear glacial kettle ponds dot this wooded parkland far removed, physically and ecologically, from the Cape's shores. Canoe and fish the ponds, watch rare songbirds, and camp at over 400 sites.

Map of Cape Cod

Provincetown

Wellfleet

Cape Cod Bay

Eastham

Sandwich

Dennis

Orleans

Buzzards Bay

Barnstable

Chatham

East Falmouth

Hyannis

South Yarmouth

Woods Hole

Falmouth

6 **Chatham**
An iconic
lighthouse marks the
dangerous shoals off
Chatham's astounding
and ever-shifting barrier
beaches, where seabirds
flock and seals bask in
the winter sun. Home to
the Cape's main tuna
fleet, Chatham is also
a yachtsmen's harbor.

7 **King's Highway**
More shady lane than highway, Route 6A
strings together the salty Cape Cod Bay villages
filled with the mansions of Victorian sea captains,
antiques dealers, and the studios of potters,
glassblowers, and other artisans.

8 **Cape Cod Rail Trail**
This is one of the most
invigorating ways to see
Cape Cod. The 22-mile
(35-km) Rail Trail begins
in Dennis, crosses fields
and forest, skirts a
quaint fishing harbor,
and then follows dune
cliffs into Wellfleet.

9 **Provincetown**
It's always party
time in P-town **(left)**.
The Cape's most colorful
community is at once a
Portuguese-American
fishing village, a major
art colony, and a leading
gay resort destination.

10 **Falmouth and Woods Hole**
Marine researchers
dominate tiny Woods
Hole **(above)**, a harbor of
professors who look like
pirates. Falmouth proper
is a quintessential New
England town of neat
houses and tall churches.

🔟 ⭐ Newport, Rhode Island

This small city packs a huge amount of history into a few square miles. Not only does it boast America's first naval college and first synagogue, its White Horse Tavern has been serving drinks since 1673. In the late 1800s, the rich began building ornate mansions along the cliffs south of the city center to escape fetid summers in New York. The New York Yacht Club made Newport its summer headquarters, and the city's harbor is home to many contenders for the America's Cup, the most prestigious match race in sailing.

1 The Breakers
Explore the gilt- and marble-encrusted interior of this 70-room Italian Renaissance-style mansion, completed in 1895, to appreciate the preeminence of the Vanderbilt family – who called it home – among the economic aristocracy of America.

2 Museum of Newport History
Artifacts and displays inside the Brick Store trace the merchants, patriots, craftsmen, and social elite of Newport with an emphasis on the 18th and 19th centuries.

3 Washington Square
Colonial-era Newport's focal point was damaged but not destroyed by British occupiers during the American Revolution. The city's oldest house (1697) is nearby **(above)**.

4 Cliff Walk
The exhilarating amble **(above)** along Newport's east-facing cliffs will have you looking two ways at once – up to the lawns of the mansions on Bellevue Avenue and down to watch surfers catching waves at Easton's Beach.

6 Fort Adams State Park
The windy point between Newport Harbor and the Narragansett Bay East Passage is perfect for watching racing sailboats or flying kites. Newport's famous jazz and folk festivals are held here.

5 America's Cup Charters Cruises
Enjoy Newport Harbor's beauty from the deck of a racing yacht **(below)** that once competed for the America's Cup. You may even get to take the wheel.

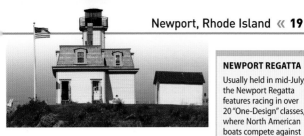

7 Rose Island and Lighthouse
Volunteers man this historic lighthouse (above) a mile offshore from Newport. Experienced paddlers kayak to the island for excellent birding.

NEWPORT REGATTA

Usually held in mid-July, the Newport Regatta features racing in over 20 "One-Design" classes, where North American boats compete against others of like design. Sailing is only half the fun – the regatta is the highlight of the summer social season that starts at the marinas and spills over into the lively bars and restaurants.

NEED TO KNOW

MAP F5

Newport Visitor Information Center: 23 America's Cup Ave; 401 845 9123; open daily

The Breakers: 44 Ochre Point Ave; 401 847 1000; open daily; adm

Museum of Newport History: 127 Thames St; 401 841 8770; open daily; adm

America's Cup Charters: 401 846 9886; open May–Oct; adm

Fort Adams State Park: Harrison Ave; 401 847 2400; open daily

Rose Island Lighthouse: 401 847 4242; open daily late May–Labor Day

Touro Synagogue: 85 Touro St; 401 847 4794; call for tour times; adm

International Tennis Hall of Fame: 194 Bellevue Ave; 401 849 3990; open daily (Feb–Mar: closed Tue); adm

■ An inexpensive RIPTA trolley day pass is the best way to see Newport.

■ Look for a truck selling Del's Lemonade along Thames Street or at Fort Adams State Park.

Map of Newport

9 International Tennis Hall of Fame
Play on the grass courts where US tournament tennis was born in 1881. The Hall still hosts professional matches played on grass. The excellent museum chronicles the sport.

8 Touro Synagogue
The oldest synagogue in America, the spare and elegant Touro Synagogue was constructed in 1763 by religious refugees from Spain and Portugal.

10 Bowen's Wharf
You could develop a nautical swagger walking Bowen's Wharf, the anchor of Newport's waterfront activity since 1760. Head here for sail or powerboat tours, shopping at boutiques, or casual and fine dining.

TOP 10 ⭐ White Mountains, New Hampshire

More than 20 summits topping 4,000 ft (1,200 m) define the rugged north country of New Hampshire, of which 1,200 sq miles (3,116 sq km) is set aside as the White Mountain National Forest. The area is ideal for some of the main outdoor activities of New England: summer hiking and climbing, fall foliage sightseeing, and winter skiing. Drive through the White Mountains to encounter soaring mountain ridges, tumbling waterfalls, deep glens, and dark forests. Wildlife abounds – be careful of deer and moose on the roads at dusk.

1 Franconia Notch State Park

Stop along this 8-mile (13-km) pass between the Franconia and Kinsman mountain ranges to hike the challenging trails of the narrow-cut Flume Gorge, with its steep rock walls and gushing waterfalls.

2 Kancamagus Highway

One of few roads across the spine of the White Mountains, the 34-mile (55-km) "Kanc" is among the state's most thrilling drives. Park the car and get out at the designated scenic areas **(above)** to picnic, hike, or explore Colonial history (see p60).

3 Mount Washington and the Cog Railway

New England's highest peak at 6,288 ft (1,917 m), Mount Washington has lured climbers and sightseers since the 1840s. For the most picturesque ascent, take a 3-hour round trip on the Cog Railway **(right)**, operating since 1869.

4 Conway Scenic Railroad

See the scenery as earlier generations did – from a train. Go through Mount Washington Valley, or over the towering trestles of Crawford Notch.

NEED TO KNOW

MAP L3–4, M3–4

Franconia Notch State Park Flume Gorge and Visitor Center: 603 745 8391; open May–Oct: daily; adm

White Mountain National Forest Saco District Ranger Station: 33 Kancamagus Hwy; 603 447 5448; open daily

Mount Washington Cog Railway: Marshfield Base Station, off Rte 302; 603 278 5404; open Apr–Nov; adm

Conway Scenic Railroad: Rte 16, North Conway; 603 356 5251; mid-Apr–Dec; adm

Pinkham Notch Visitor Center: Joe Dodge Lodge, Rte 16, north of North Conway; 603 466 2727; open daily

Whale's Tale Waterpark 491 Daniel Webster Hwy, Lincoln; 603 745 8810; open mid-Jun–Labor Day; adm

■ In foliage season, drive the "Kanc" on a weekday, when there's less traffic.

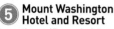

5 Mount Washington Hotel and Resort

Legendary golfing and winter skiing are just two of the draws of this palatial, old-time White Mountain resort **(above)**, which opened in 1902 *(see p148)*.

Map of the White Mountains

9 North Conway

Gateway to the east side of the White Mountains, North Conway is a bustling commercial center. Spend the morning hiking, and the afternoon cruising for discounted designer goods at more than 200 outlet stores.

10 Whale's Tale Waterpark

With water slides for every age group, wave pools, wading pools, and a river that snakes through the 17-acre (7-ha) park, Whale's Tale is New Hampshire's top aquatic attraction.

6 Ski Mountains

Sudden drops and heavy snowfall make the White Mountains a top ski destination. Cannon Mountain *(see p54)* and Wildcat Mountain have lots of summer activities. Loon Mountain has great mountain-biking trails.

8 Lincoln and Woodstock

With the Kancamagus Highway to the east and Franconia Notch to the north, Lincoln and Woodstock **(below)** are the civilized little villages that serve as easy-going base camps for hikers, climbers, skiers, and other outdoors enthusiasts.

7 Pinkham Notch

This rocky pass is a hub for backcountry skiers and hikers. Hikes range from easy walking to challenging trails in Tuckerman Ravine.

Following pages Acorn Street in Beacon Hill, Boston

TOP 10 ⭐ Litchfield Hills, Connecticut

Tucked into the northwest corner of Connecticut, the undulating Litchfield Hills are the most scenic and bucolic section of the state. Technically an extension of the Taconic Mountains and the Berkshire Hills, the region is laced with a network of mountain streams, making fly-fishing for trout a leading springtime activity. Most sizable towns nestle in the valley of the Housatonic River, and their historic homes attest to Colonial settlement and recent gentrification by wealthy New Yorkers.

1 Mount Tom State Park

Views from the summit of Mount Tom entice hikers to this modest peak – an elevation gain of only 500 ft (152 m). The park's lake is a favorite with families and scuba divers alike.

4 Kent Falls State Park

North of the village of Kent, this park is home to an impressive waterfall **(right)**, a 250-ft (76-m) drop over slate and marble. Follow the trail to the top to see the most vigorous chute of all.

6 Litchfield

Local gentry flock to this market town to shop, dine, worship, and admire the many historic homes, including the first US law school (1784).

2 Lake Waramaug

Farmland around New Preston's Lake Waramaug **(above)** is temperate enough to grow wine grapes. Stop by Hopkins Vineyard to sample the wines. A state park on the broad, scenic lake offers picnic grounds and swimming.

3 Farmington River Tubing

Chill out on a summer day by floating down the Farmington River on an inflatable tube. The 2.5-mile (4-km) course takes in gentle ripples, a segment of turbulent rapids, and a lot of idle floating.

5 Lime Rock Park

The air is charged with testosterone and motor fumes at Lime Rock race track. Races range from stock cars to road racers to formula vehicles. High-speed driving classes are offered.

Map of Litchfield Hills

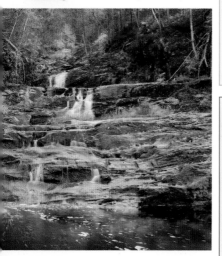

8 Shepaug Dam

In icy winter, more bald eagles **(left)** congregate at the Shepaug Dam in Southbury than almost any other place in New England. Camouflaged blinds let bird-watchers get close-up views.

NEIGHBORS WITH NAMES

The combination of Litchfield Hills' rural beauty and the easy proximity to New York City conspire to make it the home of many celebrities. Among the residents over the years have been sculptor Alexander Calder, chef Jacques Pepin, author William Styron, and a number of actors, including Meryl Streep.

NEED TO KNOW

MAP B4–5

Mount Tom State Park: Rte 202, Litchfield; 860 567 8870; open daily; adm

Farmington River Tubing: 92 Main St, New Hartford; 860 693 6465; open late May–early Sep; adm

Kent Falls State Park: Rte 7, Kent; 860 927 3238; open daily; adm

Lime Rock Park: 60 White Hollow Rd, Lakeville; 860 435 5000; open Apr–Oct; adm

Shepaug Dam Bald Eagle Observation Area: River Rd, Southbury; 860 895 6468; open late Dec–mid-Mar; bookings are required

Institute for American Indian Studies: 38 Curtis Rd, Washington; 860 868 0518; open daily; adm

■ Visit the gardens of White Flower Farm (167 Litchfield Rd, Morris; 860 567 8789) on Rte 63 south of Litchfield.

■ Eat barbecued meats at The Cookhouse in New Milford (see p101).

7 Housatonic River

As the Housatonic River approaches the covered bridge at West Cornwall, it enters a 12-mile (19-km) stretch that many rank the best fly-fishing in the eastern US. Join sportsmen from around New England trying their luck here in the spring.

9 Institute for American Indian Studies

Tucked high into the hilly woods of Washington, this facility re-creates a pre-European-contact Algonkian village. With a collection of artifacts dating back 10,000 years, it's the perfect spot to learn about the woodlands culture of northwestern Connecticut.

10 Woodbury

Join collectors and interior decorators as they scour Woodbury's 40-plus antiques dealers. In the village center, check out late-18th-century style at the historic Glebe House Museum **(left)** *(see p98).*

🔟 ⭐ Green Mountains, Vermont

The backbone of Vermont, these mountains run north-south from Quebec to the Massachusetts border, between the Champlain and Connecticut River valleys. Much of this stunning wilderness is set aside as the Green Mountain National Forest, which draws millions of visitors in every season for fishing, hiking, canoeing, mountain biking, camping, skiing, and snowshoeing. State Route 100, which runs between the east and west ranges of the Green Mountains, is among the most striking roads in the country for fall foliage.

1 Stowe and Mount Mansfield

The Von Trapps of *Sound of Music* fame settled in Stowe **(above)** because it so resembled the Austrian Alps. Hikers and skiers flock to the village at the foot of Mount Mansfield.

2 Killington

At 4,241 ft (1,292 m), Killington is the second-highest peak in these mountains and home to the largest ski resort in eastern North America (*see p54*).

COL. SETH WARNER

3 Middlebury

Prestigious Middlebury College adds sophistication to this typical New England community of Colonial homes and pointy-spired churches. Visit the old mill buildings along Otter Creek for a photogenic waterfall and shops.

4 Bennington

The Bennington Battle Monument **(left)** commemorates a major American Revolutionary War victory and provides sweeping panoramas of this southwest corner of the Green Mountains. The Bennington Museum (*see p110*) displays important folk art and Americana.

5 Hildene

This 24-room Georgian Revival house was built for Robert Todd Lincoln (1843–1926), the diplomat son of Abraham Lincoln (1809–65). Its highlights include family memorabilia and a 1,000-pipe Aeolian organ. Formal gardens influenced by a French-parterre style crown the impressive grounds.

6 Mount Equinox Skyline Drive
This 5-mile (8-km) toll road (above), along a high ridge, offers spectacular sunsets and breathtaking views of the Green, Adirondack, White, Berkshire, and Taconic mountain ranges.

7 Manchester
A genteel vacation resort since the 1890s, Manchester is so posh that its sidewalks are marble. Shop in the upscale designer outlet stores on the outskirts, or hit the slopes at nearby Stratton and Bromley ski areas.

8 Robert Frost Wayside
Poet Robert Frost (1874–1963) and the Vermont landscape where he farmed are inseparable. See nature through a poet's eyes by following the effortless interpretive trail in Ripton to a cabin where he wrote much of his later verse.

9 Mad River Valley
Tucked between two ranges of the Green Mountains, this region boasts a ski area (see p55), chic Waitsfield village, and the outdoors sports center of Warren. Historic covered bridges cross many streams.

10 The Long Trail
This 270-mile (432-km) path follows the Green Mountains from Massachusetts to Quebec, crossing most of Vermont's highest peaks. Take a day hike between access points (below).

Map of the Green Mountains

Burlington
89
7 Waterbury
Waitsfield 9
100
Middlebury 3
7 8
Brandon
Rutland Killington
4 100 2
Wallingford
30 10
6 Manchester 7
100 5
77
Bennington 4
9

NEED TO KNOW
MAP K3–6, J6

Green Mountain National Forest Manchester Ranger Station: 2538 Depot St, Manchester Center; 802 362 2307; open Mon–Fri

Bennington Battle Monument: 15 Monument Circle, Bennington; 802 447 0550; open daily mid-Apr–Oct; adm

Hildene: 1005 Hildene Rd, Manchester; 802 362 1788; open daily; adm

Green Mtn Club Visitor Center: 4711 Waterbury-Stowe Rd; 802 244 7037; open mid-May–mid-Oct: daily; mid-Oct–mid-May: Mon–Fri

■ Especially in the north, temperatures plummet in winter, spelling icy conditions. Be prepared for road closures.

■ The Warren Store (284 Main St, Warren) has hot grilled food, sandwiches, pastries, and sweets at breakfast and lunch.

★ Portland and Casco Bay, Maine

The motto of Maine's largest city is *Resurgam*, or "I shall rise again," for good reason. Portland has burned down four times since its foundation in 1633. Building codes set up after the 1866 Great Fire created a legacy of handsome Victorian structures. Redevelopment has transformed the waterfront with dining and entertainment, and former warehouses have become boutiques and galleries. A short drive from downtown lie the parks and sandy beaches of Casco Bay.

1 Victoria Mansion

Portland-born hotelier Sylvester Morse (1816–93) made his fortune in New Orleans. The elaborate Italianate manse (below) he built in 1860 as his summer home showed the folks back home how well he'd done.

2 Two Lights State Park

Sandy dunes and rocky points meet at this state park, named for a pair of 19th-century lighthouses.

3 Windjammer and Whale-Watching Cruises

You might see humpback, finback, and minke whales roll in the water, spout, and leap during a 4-hour whale-watching trip, or view Portland from Casco Bay on a 2-hour sail aboard a gaff-rigged sloop.

4 Portland Head Light and Fort Williams Park

Maine's oldest lighthouse, Portland Head (below) was built in 1791 as part of Fort Williams. This stately beacon marking the entrance to Casco Bay is one of the world's most photographed lighthouses.

5 Old Port District

The colorful shops of the Old Port District (below) range from dealers in antiques and fine crafts to coffee roasters, candy stores, and boutiques. Both fresh-caught lobsters and harbor island commuters come ashore at the docks.

6 Crescent Beach State Park

Spread out a blanket on the mile-long arc of beach, go exploring for shells, and take a dip to appreciate the soft sand and safe waters at this park, which is favored by Portland locals but little known to travelers.

Map of Portland and Casco Bay

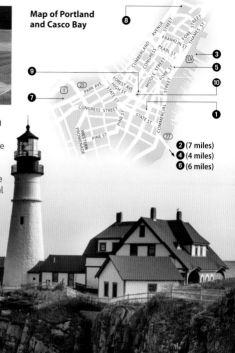

7 Portland Sea Dogs

A minor-league affiliate of major-league baseball's Boston Red Sox, the Sea Dogs have a loyal, almost fanatical following in Portland. The home games are played at Hadlock Field (above).

8 Portland Observatory

Built in 1807 to alert merchants when their ships were arriving, this 86-ft (26-m) wooden observation tower is the last remaining US maritime signal station. It provides fine views of Portland harbor.

9 Children's Museum and Theatre of Maine

An ambitious program of plays for children and interactive exhibits that both entertain and enlighten make the Children's Museum and Theatre of Maine an essential place to visit with kids up to age 12.

10 Portland Museum of Art

In a complex of three historic buildings, the museum features painters of the Maine landscape, notably Winslow Homer (1836–1910), Marsden Hartley (1877–1943), and Rockwell Kent (1882–1971) (see p40).

NEED TO KNOW

MAP N4

Two Lights State Park: Cape Elizabeth; 207 799 5871; adm

Odyssey Whale Watch: 170 Commercial St; 207 775 0727; adm

Maine Sailing Adventures: Maine State Pier, Commercial St; 207 749 9169; adm

Portland Head Light and Fort Williams Park: Shore Rd, Cape Elizabeth; 207 799 2661

Crescent Beach State Park: Rte 77, Cape Elizabeth; 207 799 5871; adm

Portland Sea Dogs: 271 Park Ave; 800 936 3647; adm

Portland Observatory: 138 Congress St; 207 774 5561; adm

Children's Museum and Theatre of Maine: 142 Free St; 207 828 1234; adm

■ Be prepared for steep walking, often on cobbles. Residential Portland is on a high ridge; downtown sits on a steep slope.

TOP10 ⭐ Lakes Region, New Hampshire

The stunning lakes dotting the high plateau and foothills south of the White Mountains began attracting settlers in the mid-18th century. Roads and railroads proliferated here in the 19th century, opening New Hampshire's lakes to tourism. There's something for everyone, from the strand of Weirs Beach to the stately grace of Wolfeboro; from the roaring racetrack in nearby Loudon to the tranquility of Squam Lake.

Lake Winni-pesaukee ①
At 21 miles (34 km) long, Winnipesaukee **(right)** is New Hampshire's largest lake. Swimmers from across the state love to congregate on its pine-clad beaches, while the more daring also race motorboats and hold waterskiing contests.

② Weirs Beach
Fun-lovers swarm this brassy resort **(below)** on the west end of Lake Winnipesaukee, where the beach and boardwalk are augmented by fairground rides, a water slide, mini-golf, souvenir shops, and all the cotton candy you can eat.

Map of the Lakes Region

Moultonborough · ㉕
⑤ Holderness · ⑥
⑧ · ㉛ · ⑨
Meredith · ⑩⑨ Ossipee · ⑯
④ · Tuftonboro
Weirs Beach · ① ·
② · Glendale · Wolfeboro · ⑦
Lakeport
Laconia · ㉘ · ⑩
⑪
③

③ M/S Mount Washington
Cruising on this 230-ft (70-m) historic vessel is the most relaxing way to see Lake Winnipesaukee; while you relax, listen to a running commentary on celebrity homes and natural attractions along the way.

④ Winnipesaukee Scenic Railroad
You never lose sight of Winnipesaukee on summer shoreline excursions between Meredith and Lakeport, with stopovers at Weirs Beach. The railroad also operates weekend fall foliage trips from Meredith or Weirs Beach.

6 Castle in the Clouds

Tour this stone castle **(left)**, set on a bluff 750 ft (229 m) above Lake Winnipesaukee. Then hike some of the 28 miles (45 km) of trails, or take a stroll to a waterfall.

7 Wolfeboro

The village, a resort destination since 1763, when the Royal Governor built a summer home here, represents the demure, gentrified side of Winnipesaukee and is the largest community on the lake.

8 Meredith

Warm-water bass fishing is one of the lures of upscale Meredith, the epicenter of tasteful resort development on Lake Winnipesaukee. Capitalizing on New Hampshire's lack of sales tax, Meredith is also the lake's premier shopping destination.

MOTORCYCLE WEEK

Tens of thousands of motorcycle enthusiasts gather in and around Laconia in mid-June for the adrenaline-charged touring, partying, and races of the Laconia Motorcycle Week, a popular annual event since 1925. Area lodging books up in advance.

9 Ossipee

Enjoy hiking, blackberry picking, and horseback riding in quiet country roads around Ossipee, set in a pond-dotted plateau just east of Lake Winnipesaukee.

10 Gunstock Mountain Resort

Born as a Depression-era public works project, Gunstock has evolved into a popular ski area. In summer, vast forests make it a favorite for outdoor pursuits.

Squam Lake 5

Best known as the loon-haunted lake of the 1981 movie *On Golden Pond*, Squam **(right)** is a natural paradise, best appreciated on a boat tour with a guide from the Squam Lakes Natural Science Center.

NEED TO KNOW

MAP M4–5

Lakes Region Association: Exit 20, Tilton; 603 286 8008

M/S Mount Washington: 211 Lakeside Ave, Weirs Beach; 603 366 5531; open late May–mid-Oct; adm

Winnipesaukee Scenic Railroad: 154 Main St, Meredith; 603 745 2135; open May–Oct; adm

Squam Lakes Natural Science Center: Rte 113, Holderness; 603 968 7194; open daily May–Oct; adm

Castle in the Clouds: Moultonborough (Rte 171); 603 476 5900; open daily Jun–mid Oct; adm

Gunstock Mountain Resort: 719 Cherry Valley Rd, Gilford; 603 293 4341; open year-round; adm

■ Catch free concerts on Saturday nights in July and August at Cate Park bandstand in Wolfeboro.

■ For dining with views of Winnipesaukee, try Patrick's Pub & Eatery (see p120).

TOP10 ⭐ Berkshires, Massachusetts

Colonial-era villages of the southern Berkshires attest to the rich soils of the Housatonic Valley, while former brick mill towns of the north hint at 19th-century industrialization. Today, though, the region's identity revolves around the summer arts scene: music, dance, theater. The natural world, too, is always alluring. Mountain laurel explodes into bloom in June, and deer browse in abandoned apple orchards. Mountaintop trails lead to sweeping views, or you can hike into deep woods where a waterfall plunges into a still pool.

3 Mount Greylock

American authors Nathaniel Hawthorne and Henry David Thoreau climbed Greylock and sang its praises. You can reach the summit, too, either via several scenic hiking trails or by car.

1 Williamstown

Williams College (above) lends a young spirit to this historic village at the edge of Mount Greylock. The Clark holds several unmissable treasures (see p41).

2 Norman Rockwell Museum

The museum (left) focuses on the popular illustrator whose works celebrate small-town American life in the mid-20th century. Changing exhibitions explore the illustration work of his edgier contemporaries.

Map of the Berkshires

NEED TO KNOW

MAP B2-3

Berkshires Visitors Bureau: 66 Allen St, Pittsfield; 413 499 1600; open Mon–Fri

Norman Rockwell Museum: 9 Rte 183, Stockbridge; 413 298 4100; open daily year-round; adm

Mount Greylock State Reservation Visitor Center: 30 Rockwell Rd, Lanesborough; 413 499 4262; open daily year-round

■ If you're looking for an easy climb, try modest Monument Mountain on Rte 7 a few miles south of Stockbridge. The roundtrip hike to the summit takes about 90 minutes.

■ Head to the deli behind Rubiner's Cheesemongers (264 Main St, Great Barrington; 413 528 0488) for gourmet sandwiches, many with exotic cheeses.

7 Jacob's Pillow Dance Festival

This woodsy mountaintop retreat in Becket is the venue for performances by top-flight dance companies from around the world, as well as workshop productions of edgy new choreography (see p81).

8 North Adams

This erstwhile factory town at the west end of the Mohawk Trail has embraced the art world and vice versa. It is best known for Mass MoCA (see p40), where provocative contemporary art fills a former factory.

9 Hancock Shaker Village

Now converted to a museum that brings the Shaker story to life, Hancock was among the most influential of 19th-century Shaker communities. Its Round Barn is considered to be a masterpiece of vernacular architecture (see p39).

4 Stockbridge

American illustrator Norman Rockwell (1894–1978) modeled his nostalgic treatments of rural American life on the people and buildings of this slow-paced village (above), dominated by the Red Lion Inn.

5 Lenox

A quaint village surrounded by grand houses and vast estates largely built as summer "cottages" between 1880 and 1910, Lenox is the epicenter of luxury shopping and the summer performing arts scene.

6 Great Barrington

A vibrant mix of artists, artisans, savvy business folk, and New Age visionaries makes Great Barrington easily the hippest town in the Berkshires, as well as a gateway to antiques shopping on Route 7 south of town.

10 Tanglewood Music Center

The summer home of the Boston Symphony Orchestra (below) since 1940, Tanglewood Music Center also hosts jazz, chamber music, and popular music concerts, and in summer operates an important music education program.

The Top 10 of Everything

**Courtyard at Isabella Stewart
Gardner Museum, Boston**

Moments in History

1 **10000 BC–AD 1000: Settlement**
As glaciers retreated from New England some 12,000 years ago, hunters moved in. By AD 1000, they lived in seasonal villages and farming augmented hunting and fishing. Most spoke an Algonkian language; their dialects persist on Native lands in Massachusetts, Maine, and Connecticut.

2 **1620: Colonization**
Religious reformers from England swarmed into New England; first the Pilgrims at Plymouth, Massachusetts (1620), then Puritan colonies at Salem (1626) and Boston (1630). Soon communities were springing up in Rhode Island, Connecticut, and New Hampshire.

Painting depicting the Revolution

3 **1775: Revolution**
Tensions between mother country and colonies came to a head in 1775 with the occupation of Boston. On April 19, British redcoats and American rebels exchanged fire in Lexington and Concord. Within weeks, the American Revolution had begun.

Whale hunting, New Bedford

4 **1785: Trade with China**
In 1785, merchants from Salem, Massachusetts, opened China to American trade. By 1845, shipbuilders in New England had developed the Yankee clipper, a swift sailing vessel that dominated the China trade well into the 1860s.

5 **1799–1821: Industrialization and Manufacturing**
From 1799 to 1813, Eli Whitney's Connecticut gun plants pioneered interchangeable parts and the assembly line. In 1821, textile entrepreneurs brought the Industrial Revolution to Lowell, Massachusetts, complete with purloined English loom designs and a factory-city scheme that was quickly replicated throughout the region.

6 **1820–60: Whaling Hegemony**
In the 1700s, Nantucket Islanders were among the first to hunt whales around the globe. The whale-oil business proved immensely lucrative, justifying larger ships and longer voyages. New Bedford, Massachusetts, was the world capital of whaling from the 1820s until the 1960s, when petroleum displaced whale oil.

7 **1861–5: Abolition and the Civil War**
New England led the fight to abolish slavery in the United States. The

region harbored fugitive slaves, and abolition societies flourished in both black and white communities. New Englanders volunteered in overwhelming numbers to fight for the Union in the Civil War (1861–5), which decimated many rural areas.

⑧ 1865–1900: The Gilded Age

In the late 19th century, great wealth was generated as railroads spanned the country, industry expanded exponentially, and immigrants flowed into the country to fill job openings.

⑨ 1890–1950: The Rise of Tourism

Railroad construction opened the mountains and coasts of New England to scenic tourism. After World War II, new highways and roadside motels brought multitudes of new visitors to Cape Cod, the Maine coast, and the White and Green Mountains.

The Conway railroad, White Mountains

⑩ 1960–Today: Education and the Knowledge Economy

The founding of Harvard College in 1636 is what gave New England a head start in higher education. The emphasis on scholarship has persisted down the years, and has produced industrial leaders in such fields as information technology, robotics, and biotechnology.

TOP 10 REFORMERS AND REVOLUTIONARIES

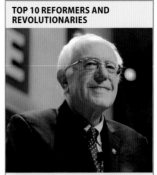

US politician Bernie Sanders

1 Dorothea Dix (1802–87)
Advocate for the mentally ill, Dix also led Union Army nursing in the Civil War.

2 William Lloyd Garrison (1805–79)
Garrison edited the radical newspaper *The Liberator* and co-founded the American Anti-Slavery Society.

3 Joseph Smith (1805–44)
Vermont-born visionary Joseph Smith founded Mormonism.

4 Harriet Beecher Stowe (1811–96)
Prominent abolitionist Stowe attacked slavery in her famous 1852 novel, *Uncle Tom's Cabin*.

5 Clara Barton (1821–1912)
Nurse, teacher, and suffragist, Barton founded the US branch of the International Red Cross.

6 Mary Baker Eddy (1821–1910)
Eddy was the founder of the Christian Science movement.

7 Justice Oliver Wendell Holmes Jr. (1841–1935)
This Supreme Court Justice was noted for his blunt and pithy opinions.

8 W.E.B. DuBois (1868–1963)
A sociologist, scholar, and activist, DuBois was among the 20th century's most prominent civil rights leaders.

9 Benjamin Spock (1903–98)
Pediatrician Spock shook up American child-rearing by emphasizing affection over discipline.

10 Bernie Sanders (b. 1941)
Progressive Vermont politician Sanders restored credibility to the American Left in the 2016 presidential nomination run.

TOP 10 Colonial and Historic Sites

1 Old Sturbridge Village, MA

MAP D3 ▪ Rte 20, Sturbridge ▪ 508 347 3362 ▪ Open mid-May–Oct: 9:30am–5pm daily; call for winter hours ▪ Adm ▪ www.osv.org

Heritage livestock breeds and costumed guides create a vivid sense of New England rural life in the early 19th century at this living history museum. The village features more than 40 historic buildings moved from across the region.

Minute Man statue

2 Strawbery Banke, NH

MAP N6 ▪ 14 Hancock St, Portsmouth ▪ 603 433 1100 ▪ Open May–Oct: 10am–5pm daily; Nov–Dec: call for tour hours ▪ Adm ▪ www.strawberybanke.org

Follow the development and growth of Portsmouth, NH, in this complex of historic dwellings assembled at Strawbery Banke, the city's original settlement. Period furnishings and historical gardens help to chronicle the daily life of the seaside city from the 17th to the 20th century.

3 Plimoth Plantation, MA

MAP G3 ▪ 137 Warren Ave, Plymouth ▪ 508 746 1622 ▪ Open late Mar–Nov: 9am–5pm daily ▪ Adm ▪ www.plimoth.org

Step back in time to 1627 at Plimoth Plantation, where costumed inter-preters speaking 17th-century English portray original settlers inside the stockaded village so studiously that references to modern life are met with quizzical looks. There are Native American interpreters on hand at the re-created Wampanoag encampment.

4 Minute Man National Historical Park, MA

MAP E2 ▪ North Bridge Visitor Center: 174 Liberty St, Concord; 978 369 6993 ▪ Open daily (visitor center open Apr–Oct: 9:30am–5:30pm daily; call for winter hours) ▪ www.nps.gov/mima

On April 19, 1775, British troops engaged Colonial rebels in Lexington and Concord. This opening salvo of the American Revolution sent the British into retreat and galvanized other colonies to take up arms. Exhibits and annual reenactments depict a stirring historical moment.

5 Billings Farm & Museum, VT

MAP K5 ▪ 5302 River Rd, Woodstock ▪ 802 457 2355 ▪ Open May–Oct: 10am–5pm daily; Nov–Feb: 10am–4pm Sat–Sun ▪ Adm ▪ www.billingsfarm.org

Set up in 1871, Billings Farm was turned into a museum of rural life in 1982. Its rolling green pastures and fine farm buildings represent the ideal of Vermont dairy farming. Interact with sheep, horses, and chickens, and watch the herd of Jersey cows being milked.

Plimoth Plantation

6 Slater Mill, RI

MAP E4 ■ 67 Roosevelt Ave, Pawtucket ■ 401 725 8638 ■ Open Mar–Apr & Nov: 11am–3pm Sat–Sun; May–Jun & Sep–Oct: 10am–4pm Tue–Sun; Jul–Aug: 10am–4pm daily ■ Adm ■ www.slatermill.org

Dating from 1793, Slater Mill was the first successful cotton-spinning mill in the United States. The ingenuity of the early machinery, which was driven by water power transmitted through giant flapping leather belts, will fascinate engineering buffs.

Canterbury Shaker Village

7 Canterbury Shaker Village, NH

MAP M5 ■ 288 Shaker Rd, Canterbury ■ 603 783 9511 ■ Open mid-May–Oct: 10am–5pm daily; call for winter tour hours ■ Adm ■ www.shakers.org

Founded in 1792, Canterbury was a working Shaker village into the 1960s. Demonstrations and workshops teach you about Shaker skills and ideals, while informative daily tours of original Shaker buildings include fond anecdotes of the sect's final generation.

8 Weir Farm National Historic Site, CT

MAP B6 ■ 735 Nod Hill Rd, Wilton ■ 203 834 1896 ■ Open May–Oct: 10am–4pm; grounds open dawn–dusk year-round ■ www.nps.gov/wefa

The painter J. Alden Weir (1852–1919) made this rustic farm into a retreat for himself and his friends at the end of the 19th century. Two more generations of artists worked here before the property passed into the care of the National Park Service.

9 Hancock Shaker Village, MA

MAP B2 ■ 1843 W. Housatonic St, Rte 20, Pittsfield ■ 413 443 0188 ■ Open mid-Apr–late Jun: 10am–4pm daily; late Jun–Oct: 10am–5pm daily ■ Adm ■ www.hancockshakervillage.org

Learn about the artful skills of the Shakers at this settlement founded in 1790. The iconic 1826 Round Stone Barn perfectly encapsulates their ability for making things both functional and beautiful.

10 Lowell National Historical Park, MA

MAP F2 ■ Visitor Center: 246 Market St, Lowell; 978 970 5000 ■ Open mid-Mar–Nov: 9am–5pm daily; call for winter and tour hours ■ Adm ■ www.nps.gov/lowe

Lowell launched the Industrial Revolution in the United States, and this urban park preserves the city's network of canals and many of its 19th-century textile mills. The racket of the mighty water-powered looms operating in the 1864 Boott Cotton Mill gives a real sense of what it was like to work here.

🔟 Art Museums

Isabella Stewart Gardner Museum

① Isabella Stewart Gardner Museum, Boston, MA

MAP S6 ■ 25 Evans Way ■ 617 566 1401 ■ Open 11am–5pm Wed, Fri–Mon, 11am–9pm Thu ■ Adm
■ www.gardnermuseum.org

One of the all-time great private collectors, Gardner built this lovely Renaissance-style palace to display her 2,500-object collection.

② Mass MoCA, North Adams, MA

MAP B2 ■ 1040 Mass MoCA Way ■ 413 662 2111 ■ Open late Jun–Labor Day: 10am–6pm Sun–Wed (to 7pm Thu–Sat); Sep–late Jun: 11am–5pm Wed–Mon ■ Adm ■ www.massmoca.org

The Mass MoCA museum focuses on new work by living artists, and also stages dance, avant-garde theater, and performance art.

③ Portland Museum of Art, Portland, ME

MAP N4 ■ 7 Congress Sq ■ 207 775 6148 ■ Open 10am–5pm Tue–Sun (to 9pm Fri); 10am–5pm Mon (end May–mid-Oct) ■ Adm
■ www.portlandmuseum.org

A visit to Maine's largest art museum is rewarded by the chance to admire the work of the great American landscape painters, including Winslow Homer, Fitz Henry Lane, and Marsden Hartley.

④ Worcester Art Museum, MA

MAP E3 ■ 55 Salisbury St ■ 508 799 4406 ■ Open 11am–5pm Wed–Fri, Sun, 10am–5pm Sat ■ Adm
■ www.worcesterart.org

Striking Roman mosaics, arms and armor, and a top collection of pre-Columbian art from Mexico and Central America are the highlights at this small general art museum.

⑤ Currier Museum of Art, Manchester, NH

MAP M6 ■ 150 Ash St ■ 603 669 6144 ■ Open 11am–5pm Sun–Mon, Wed–Fri, 10am–5pm Sat ■ Adm
■ www.currier.org

In addition to its emphasis on 19th-century painting, the Currier Museum's collection embraces dynamic contemporary art as well.

⑥ Museum of Fine Arts, Boston, MA

MAP S6 ■ 465 Huntington Ave ■ 617 267 9300 ■ Open 10am–5pm Mon–Tue, Sat–Sun, 10am–10pm Wed–Fri ■ Adm ■ www.mfa.org

Highlights at Boston's world-class Museum of Fine Arts (MFA) include major holdings of Asian, Egyptian, and Nubian art. It also has the most important Monet collection outside of Paris.

Homer's *The Blue Boat* at Boston's MFA

7 Peabody Essex Museum, Salem, MA

MAP F2 ▪ East India Sq ▪ 978 745 9500 ▪ Open 10am–5pm Tue–Sun ▪ Adm ▪ www.pem.org

Staggering collections of China Trade treasures, historic furniture, and Asian art and artifacts fill this soaring building by top architect Moshe Safdie.

8 The Clark, Williamstown, MA

MAP B2 ▪ 225 South St ▪ 413 458 2303 ▪ Open 10am–5pm daily ▪ Adm ▪ www.clarkart.edu

French Impressionists and English landscape artists are at the core of this diversified collection.

Avery Court, Wadsworth Atheneum

9 Wadsworth Atheneum, Hartford, CT

MAP C4 ▪ 600 Main St ▪ 860 278 2670 ▪ Open 11am–5pm Wed–Fri, 10am–5pm Sat–Sun ▪ Adm ▪ www.wadsworthatheneum.org

America's oldest public art museum has New England's best collection of the startlingly oversized landscapes of the Hudson River School.

10 Shelburne Museum, VT

MAP J3 ▪ Rte 7, Shelburne ▪ 802 985 3346 ▪ Open May–Dec: 10am–5pm daily; Jan–Apr: 10am–5pm Wed–Sun ▪ Adm ▪ www.shelburnemuseum.org

From elaborately stitched quilts to two elaborate miniature circuses, the museum celebrates American folk art and ingenuity.

TOP 10 ARTISTS OF NEW ENGLAND

Sculptor Louise Nevelson

1 John Singleton Copley (1738–1815)
America's first great portraitist, Bostonian Copley fled to England during the Revolution.

2 Fitz Henry Lane (1805–65)
Largely self-tutored, Gloucester-based Lane revolutionized the handling of light in seascapes.

3 Winslow Homer (1836–1910)
Homer is most celebrated for his vigorous Maine seascapes.

4 Childe Hassam (1859–1935)
Hassam painted the streets of Boston and the Connecticut landscape with equal flourish.

5 Marsden Hartley (1877–1943)
Hartley painted powerful abstract landscapes of his native Maine.

6 Edward Hopper (1882–1967)
While spending his summers on the coast, Hopper painted scenes full of psychological nuance.

7 Rockwell Kent (1882–1971)
Painter and illustrator Kent is best known for his stark Arctic landscapes.

8 Norman Rockwell (1894–1978)
Rockwell championed home-spun American values in covers for *The Saturday Evening Post*.

9 Louise Nevelson (1899–1988)
Raised in Maine, Nevelson is known for her Abstract Expressionist sculptural assemblages.

10 Andrew Wyeth (1917–2009)
Visual artist Wyeth is noted for the almost photographic realism of his *tempera* landscapes.

TOP 10 University Museums

① Smith College Museum of Art, Northampton, MA

MAP C3 ▪ 20 Elm St ▪ 413 585 2760 ▪ Open 10am–4pm Tue–Sat, noon–4pm Sun ▪ Adm ▪ www.smith.edu/artmuseum

Since its founding in the 1870s, Smith has collected contemporary art. Rufino Tamayo's *Nature and the Artist: The Work of Art and the Observer*, commissioned by the college in 1943, offers a rare chance to see a work by one of Mexico's leading muralists.

② Yale University Art Museums, New Haven, CT

MAP C5 ▪ Yale Center for British Art: 1080 Chapel St; 203 432 2800; open 10am–5pm Tue–Sat, noon–5pm Sun; britishart.yale.edu ▪ Yale University Art Gallery: 1111 Chapel St; 203 432 0600; open 10am–5pm Tue–Fri, 11am–5pm Sat–Sun; artgallery.yale.edu

The largest collection of British art outside the UK is kept at the Yale Center for British Art, designed by modernist architect Louis B. Kahn (1901–74). The Yale University Art Gallery, an earlier Kahn building of 1953, is noted for its American paintings and decorative arts.

Exhibit, Harvard Art Museums

③ Harvard Art Museums, Cambridge, MA

MAP F2 ▪ 32 Quincy St ▪ 617 495 9400 ▪ Open 10am–5pm daily ▪ Adm ▪ www.harvardartmuseums.org

One of the world's most wide-ranging university art museums, this boasts outstanding collections of ancient Greek, medieval, Renaissance, Impressionist, Expressionist, and Asian art.

④ Colby College Museum of Art, Waterville, ME

MAP P3 ▪ 5600 Mayflower Hill Dr ▪ 207 859 5600 ▪ Open 10am–5pm Tue–Sat, noon–5pm Sun ▪ www.colby.edu/museum

An excellent survey of major American artists is capped with key holdings of modern and contemporary artists associated with Maine, including Marsden Hartley (1877–1943) and Alex Katz (b. 1927).

⑤ Peary-MacMillan Arctic Museum, Brunswick, ME

MAP P4 ▪ Hubbard Hall ▪ Bowdoin College ▪ 207 725 3416 ▪ Open 10am–5pm Tue–Sat, 2–5pm Sun ▪ www.bowdoin.edu/arctic-museum

Named for Bowdoin College alumni Robert E. Peary (1856–1920) and Donald B. MacMillan (1874–1970), this museum brings their daring Arctic explorations to life. Natural history specimens, Inuit artifacts, and photographs offer insight on the cultures of the far north.

⑥ RISD Museum, Providence, RI

MAP E4 ▪ 224 Benefit St ▪ 401 454 6500 ▪ Open 10am–5pm Tue–Sun, 10am–9pm third Thu of the month ▪ Adm ▪ www.risdmuseum.org

Students at New England's top art and design school seek inspiration here. The historically

Yale Center for British Art

Manet's *Le Repos*, RISD Museum

encyclopedic collection of more than 84,000 objects is notable for late-19th-century painting (including French Impressionism), as well as post-1960 arts in various media. Contemporary studio crafts and furniture are also strong. Early American furniture stars in the decorative arts wing.

7 Hood Museum of Art, Hanover, NH

MAP L4 ▪ Dartmouth College ▪ 603 646 2808 ▪ Closed until 2019 for renovation and expansion ▪ www. hoodmuseum.dartmouth.edu

With over 65,000 works, Assyrian stone reliefs from the palace of Ashurnasirpal (around 900 BC) are the Hood's prize display. Strong selections of Native American, sub-Saharan, and Melanesian art bring a global sweep to the galleries.

8 Ballard Institute and Museum of Puppetry, Storrs, CT

MAP D4 ▪ 1 Royce Circle, Suite 101B, University of Connecticut ▪ 860 486 8580 ▪ Open 11am–7pm Tue–Sun ▪ Donation ▪ www.bimp.uconn.edu

The key exhibits at this unique puppetry museum, one of America's largest, are the puppets of Frank

Ballard (1929–2010), a drama professor who set up America's first degree course in puppetry.

9 Harvard Museum of Natural History, Cambridge, MA

MAP F2 ▪ 26 Oxford St ▪ 617 495 3045 ▪ Open 9am–5pm daily ▪ Adm ▪ www.hmnh.harvard.edu

As the public face of three Harvard research institutions, this museum combines the charm of old-fashioned artifacts with cutting-edge science. The Glass Flowers are famous worldwide for their utterly realistic re-creation of plants and blossoms. Dinosaur skeletons, gemstones, and meteorites invariably elicit awe.

10 Culinary Arts Museum at Johnson & Wales University, Providence, RI

MAP E4 ▪ 315 Harborside Blvd ▪ 401 598 2805 ▪ Open 10am–5pm Tue–Sat ▪ Adm ▪ www.culinary.org

This small museum of the culinary arts and hospitality industry will delight, with its historic roadside diners, fascinating kitchen gadgets, and even a rundown on state and presidential dinners. See how the hierarchy of the professional kitchen developed, and learn about great chefs through the ages.

TOP10 Personal Museums

① John F. Kennedy Presidential Library and Museum, Boston, MA

MAP F3 ▪ Columbia Point ▪ 617 514 1600 ▪ Open 9am–5pm daily ▪ Adm ▪ www.jfklibrary.org

This museum not only chronicles JFK's 1,000 days in office, it also touches on the man behind the myth.

John F. Kennedy Library and Museum

② Orchard House, Concord, MA

MAP E2 ▪ 399 Lexington Rd ▪ 978 369 4118 ▪ Open Apr–Oct: 10am–4:30pm Mon–Sat, 1–4:30pm Sun; Nov–Mar: 11am–3pm Mon–Fri, 10am–4:30pm Sat, 1–4:30pm Sun ▪ Adm ▪ www.louisamayalcott.org

Louisa May Alcott (1832–88) not only set her 1868 classic *Little Women* in Orchard House, she also wrote it here.

③ Longfellow House–Washington's Headquarters National Historic Site, Cambridge, MA

MAP F2 ▪ 105 Brattle St ▪ 617 876 4491 ▪ Open late-May–Oct: 9:30am–5pm Wed–Sun ▪ www.nps.gov/long

A visit to the home of poet Henry Wadsworth Longfellow (1807–82), one of America's most influential literary figures, lays bare both his triumphs and his tragedies, such as the fire that killed his wife and so scarred his face that he grew his signature beard.

④ Saint-Gaudens National Historic Site, Cornish, NH

MAP L5 ▪ Rte 12A ▪ 603 675 2175 ▪ Open late May–Oct: 9am–4:30pm daily; grounds open all year ▪ Adm ▪ www.nps.gov/saga

This house museum evokes the rustic idyll of the art colony that grew up around Augustus Saint-Gaudens (1848–1907), who was America's leading sculptor of the Beaux-Arts generation.

⑤ Robert Frost Farm, Derry, NH

MAP M6 ▪ 122 Rockingham Rd ▪ 603 432 3091 ▪ Open May–mid-Oct: 10am–4pm Wed–Sun (Jul–Aug daily) ▪ Adm ▪ www.robertfrostfarm.org

Young poet Robert Frost found his voice while living here from 1900 to 1911, and began writing the verse set in the New England countryside that would win him four Pulitzer Prizes and the admiration of a nation.

⑥ The Mount, Lenox, MA

MAP B3 ▪ 2 Plunkett St ▪ 413 551 5111 ▪ Open early May–Oct: 10am–5pm daily ▪ Adm ▪ www.edithwharton.org

This beautiful Berkshires estate in the gracious village of Lenox dates from 1902 and showcases the design and decorating sensibilities of literary giant Edith Wharton.

Wharton's boudoir at The Mount

⑦ Chesterwood, Stockbridge, MA

MAP B3 ▪ 4 Williamsville Rd
▪ 413 298 3579 ▪ Open late May–
mid-Oct: 10am–5pm daily ▪ Adm
▪ www.chesterwood.org

The home and studio of Daniel
Chester French (1850–1931) vividly
recalls the sculptor best known
for his seated Abraham Lincoln in
Washington, D.C.'s Lincoln Memorial.

⑧ Mark Twain House, Hartford, CT

MAP C4 ▪ 351 Farmington Ave
▪ 860 247 0998 ▪ Open 9:30am–
5:30pm daily (Feb: closed Tue) ▪ Adm
▪ www.marktwainhouse.org

Tiffany interiors feature in the
home of the great storyteller.
The adjoining museum revolves
around Twain (1835–1910) and his
contemporaries.

Romance of Autumn at Farnsworth

⑨ Farnsworth Art Museum, Rockland, ME

MAP Q3 ▪ 16 Museum St ▪ 207 596
6457 ▪ Open Jun–Oct: 10am–5pm daily;
Nov–Dec & Apr–May: 10am–5pm Tue–
Sun; Jan–Mar: 10am–4pm Wed–Sun ▪
Adm ▪ www.farnsworth museum.org

The art dynasty of N. C. (1882–1945),
Andrew (1917–2009), and James
Wyeth (b.1946) is celebrated here.

⑩ Gropius House, Lincoln, MA

MAP F2 ▪ 68 Baker Bridge Rd ▪ 781
259 8098 ▪ Open 11am–4pm Wed–Sun
(mid-Oct–May: Sat–Sun only) ▪ Adm
▪ www.historicnewengland.org

Explore the family residence of the
highly influential architect Walter
Gropius (1883–1969).

TOP 10 NEW ENGLAND BOOKS

Acclaimed novelist John Irving

1 Walden by Henry David Thoreau
Thoreau's philosophical musings in
the Massachusetts woods remain a
key text in American thought.

**2 Country of the Pointed Firs by
Sarah Orne Jewett**
Revolutionary psychological novel
about women in rural coastal Maine,
first published 1896.

**3 Outermost House by Henry
Beston**
Account of a year living on Cape
Cod's Great Beach.

4 New Hampshire by Robert Frost
This Pulitzer Prize-winning poetry
collection contains much of Frost's
most quoted verse.

**5 Hotel New Hampshire by
John Irving**
Comic turns abound in this literary
novel of despair and redemption at
an old resort hotel.

6 Mystic River by Dennis Lehane
Lehane's *noir* fiction reveals seamy
undercurrents of life on the edge
in South Boston.

**7 Little Women by Louisa May
Alcott**
The four March girls struggle to
overcome character flaws.

8 Charlotte's Web by E. B. White
Children's classic fiction finds
philosophy in the barnyard.

**9 Witches of Eastwick by
John Updike**
Women of a fictional Rhode Island
town dabble in the occult in this
parable of love and power.

10 Mortal Friends by James Carroll
The tale of Colman Brady, part Irish
revolutionary, part Boston mobster.

🔟 Maritime Sites

Skeleton, Nantucket Whaling Museum

① Nantucket Whaling Museum, Nantucket, MA

MAP H5 ■ 13 Broad St ■ 508 228 1894 ■ Open late May–Oct: 10am–5pm daily; call for winter hours ■ Adm ■ www.nha.org

Partially set in a former whale-oil refinery and candle factory, this museum tells how one small island dominated a lucrative industry for nearly a century. A 46-ft (14-m) sperm whale skeleton suspended from the ceiling sets the tone.

② Mystic Seaport, CT

MAP D5 ■ 75 Greenmanville Ave, Mystic ■ 860 572 0711 ■ Open Apr–Oct: 9am–5pm daily; Nov: 10am–4pm daily; Dec & mid-Feb–Mar: 10am–4pm Thu–Sun ■ Adm ■ www.mysticseaport.org

Walk the decks of a tall ship, or see carpenters replank a vessel at this "museum of America and the sea." Mystic Seaport replicates a 19th-century coastal village with craftspeople plying their trades, historic vessels, and a working shipyard.

Tall ship, Mystic Seaport

③ New Bedford Whaling National Historical Park, New Bedford, MA

MAP F4 ■ 33 William St ■ 508 996 4095 ■ Open 9am–5pm daily (Jan–Mar: closed Mon & Tue ■ Adm ■ www.nps.gov/nebe

In the 19th century, New Bedford was the world's leading whaling port. Many buildings of the era, including the Seamen's Bethel chapel mentioned in Herman Melville's *Moby-Dick*, have been preserved at this park. Don't miss the extraordinary scrimshaw carvings and a half-scale whaling ship at the New Bedford Whaling Museum.

④ Penobscot Marine Museum, Searsport, ME

MAP Q3 ■ 2 Church St ■ 207 548 2529 ■ Open late May–mid-Oct: 10am–5pm Mon–Sat, noon–5pm Sun ■ Adm ■ www.penobscotmarinemuseum.org

Tiny Searsport was home to 10 percent of America's deep-water sea captains by the close of the 19th century. Recapture the adventure of that time with captains' chests from the China Trade, a whale's jaw, and a wall of portraits of some 300 Searsport sea captains.

⑤ Maine Maritime Museum, Bath, ME

MAP P4 ■ 243 Washington St ■ 207 443 1316 ■ Open 9:30am–5pm daily ■ Adm ■ www.mainemaritimemuseum.org

Ships have been built at the mouth of the Kennebec River for more than three centuries. At Maine Maritime Museum, sail-era artifacts, paintings of historic vessels, and displays of Maine maritime life chronicle both the practicalities and the romance of that trade.

6 Maine Lighthouse Museum, Rockland, ME

MAP Q3 ▪ 1 Park Dr ▪ 207 594 3301 ▪ Open May–Nov: 10am–5pm Mon–Fri, 10am–4pm Sat–Sun; Nov–April: by appointment ▪ Adm ▪ www.mainelighthouse museum.org

This is one of the world's largest collections of lighthouse artifacts. Marvel at gigantic prisms that made small lamps visible far out at sea, and learn how keepers lived.

7 Salem Maritime National Historic Site, Salem, MA

MAP F2 ▪ 2 Liberty St ▪ 978 740 1650 ▪ Open Mar–Nov: 9am–5pm daily ▪ Adm ▪ www.nps. gov/sama

Salem's merchants brought the riches of the Far East back home. Uncover their fascinating story by retracing their steps along the historic wharves.

8 Historic Ship Nautilus and the Submarine Force Museum, Groton, CT

MAP D5 ▪ 1 Crystal Lake Rd ▪ 860 694 3174 ▪ Open May–Sep: 9am–5pm Wed–Mon; Oct–Apr: 9am–4pm Wed–Mon ▪ www. ussnautilus.org

Take a tour around the world's first nuclear-powered vessel and learn about the first submarine to dive

Gold coin excavated by Expedition Whydah

20,000 leagues under the sea. Visitors can try commanding the sub at simulated controls.

9 Expedition Whydah, Provincetown, MA

MAP H3 ▪ 16 MacMillan Wharf ▪ 508 487 8899 ▪ Open daily mid-Apr–Jun, Sep–Oct: 10am–5pm; Jul–Aug: 10am–6pm ▪ Adm ▪ www.whydah.com

"Black Sam" Bellamy went down with his ship in a storm off Cape Cod in April 1717. Particularly popular with youngsters, this dockside display bristles with discoveries from the ongoing excavation of the wreck, including a hoard of authentic pirate treasure.

10 Lake Champlain Maritime Museum, Vergennes, VT

MAP J4 ▪ 4472 Basin Harbor Rd ▪ 802 475 2022 ▪ Open late May–mid-Oct: 10am–5pm daily ▪ Adm ▪ www.lcmm.org

Relics from the more than 200 ships that have been wrecked on Lake Champlain are displayed here. Full-size working replicas of historic vessels help to bring the lake's boating history alive.

TOP 10 Villages

1 Old Lyme, CT
MAP D5

If Old Lyme was not actually the cradle of American Impressionism, it was at least the art movement's summer camp from 1899 into the 1930s. Surprisingly little of either the landscape or the town has changed since that artistic heyday. Unlock the history with a visit to the Florence Griswold Museum *(see p98)*, where many of the artists lodged.

2 Tiverton Four Corners, RI

The crossroads at the center of rural Tiverton on the east side of Narragansett Bay is filled with boutiques, antiques shops, and art galleries set in largely 18th-century buildings. The surrounding countryside is noted for its handsome historical stone walls and pastoral landscapes. The town also boasts an outstanding ice-cream stand, an excellent bakery, and a gourmet shop featuring local products *(see p88)*.

3 Grafton, VT

This genteel village bunched around a 200-year-old tavern epitomizes rustic Vermont charm. Grafton Village Cheese Company makes top Vermont cheddars *(see p108)*.

Entrance to the old tavern, Grafton

Colonial architecture, Wethersfield

4 Wethersfield, CT
Webb-Deane-Stevens Museum: 211 Main St, Wethersfield, CT; 860 569 0612; open May–Oct; adm; www.webb-deane-stevens.org

Founded in 1634 as one of the three original settlements in Connecticut, Wethersfield remains an enclave of some of the most striking Colonial structures in the country – although architecture buffs can get equally excited about the distinctive early 20th-century Hubbard Bungalows. A visit to the three 18th-century homes of the Webb-Deane-Stevens Museum provides visitors with an interesting insight into the roots of the Colonial Revival movement in American style *(see p95)*.

5 Wiscasset, ME
Nickels-Sortwell House: 121 Main St, Wiscasset, ME; 207 882 7169; open Jun–mid-Oct; adm; www.historicnewengland.org

A thriving shipbuilding town in the 18th and 19th centuries, Wiscasset immodestly claims to be the "prettiest village in Maine." With baronial sea captains' homes that define the Federal style, a charming waterfront, and a generous sprinkling of boutiques and restaurants, it just might be. The 1807 Nickels-Sortwell House, built for a wealthy ship owner, recaptures Wiscasset's glorious past *(see p124)*.

6 New London, NH
MAP L5

Without the overhead power lines and asphalt on the roads, New London would look as if time had stopped around 1850. Home to Colby-Sawyer College, a prestigious liberal arts school, New London bustles during the summer as the shopping and dining center for Lake Sunapee vacationers; another draw is the Barn Playhouse's summer stock theater season.

7 Kingfield, ME
MAP N2 ■ Stanley Museum: 40 School St, Kingfield, ME; 207 265 2729; open year round; adm; www.stanleymuseum.org

Gateway to the Sugarloaf ski resort *(see p55)*, this characterful mountain village is a favorite with outdoors enthusiasts. The Stanley Museum chronicles the achievements of twin native sons Francis Edgar and Freelan Oscar Stanley, best known for inventing the steam-powered Stanley Steamer cars. Their sister Chansonetta's documentary photographs capture rural life.

8 Harrisville, NH
MAP L6

This charming New England mill village has revived the production of yarn and textiles using water power. Picturesque structures include the 1838 general store, historic brick mills, and several wooden workers' cottages. It is the only early 19th-century industrial community in New England still perfectly preserved in its original form. Keen knitters will want to visit the yarn factory and shop.

9 Watch Hill, RI

The gingerbread architecture of Westerly's seaside village of Watch Hill reveals its Victorian roots – there's even a Victorian tea shop – but sport fishermen come here for the perfect confluence of surf and shoreline currents *(see p88)*.

10 Shelburne Falls, MA
MAP C2

Many artisans, musicians, and Sixties counterculture holdouts make their homes in this quirky village on the Mohawk Trail *(see p60)*. Cross the Deerfield River – which divides the town – on the Bridge of Flowers, a former railroad trestle heavily planted in blooms. The geological curiosity of glacial potholes scoured by a natural falls made the spot famous centuries ago.

Bridge of Flowers, Shelburne Falls

🔟 Islands

① Monhegan Island, ME

Every seagull, twig, and moss-covered rock on Monhegan must have been depicted in an artwork over the century or so since this fishing outpost off midcoast Maine became a summer art colony. Once the summer folk have gone, the fishermen return *(see p127)*.

A settlement on Monhegan Island

② Nantucket Island, MA

MAP H5 ■ Hyline Cruises: Ocean St Dock, Hyannis; 508 778 2600; www.hylinecruises.com

Thirty miles (48 km) off Cape Cod, Nantucket made its name through adventurous whaling and austere Quaker businessmen, who set the style with modest shingled homes. Pristine beaches, fascinating museums, and upscale shopping are among its present-day attractions.

③ Block Island, RI

Between Long Island and the Rhode Island coast, this tiny island looks like a tintype of a Victorian resort. Its beaches, nature reserves, and historic lighthouses are best explored on a bike *(see p88)*.

④ Isles of Shoals, NH

MAP N6 ■ Portsmouth Harbor Cruises, Ceres St Dock; 603 436 8084; Jun–early Sep: Tue–Fri; adm; www.portsmouthharbor.com

These nine unforested rocky islands stand so far offshore that they were first used by English, Basque, and Breton fishermen as camps to dry their catch in the summer sun.

⑤ Mount Desert Island, ME

Shaped like a baseball mitt, this big island is home to the summer resort town of Bar Harbor *(see p14)* and the unspoiled paradise of Acadia National Park.

⑥ Isle au Haut, ME

MAP R4 ■ Isle au Haut Boat Services: Seabreeze Ave, Stonington; 207 367 5193; www.isleauhaut.com

With primeval quaking bogs along the forested park trails and wild, wave-pounded bluffs, this craggy rock a few miles from Stonington offers the attractions of Mount Desert Island without the crowds.

⑦ Thimble Islands, CT

MAP C6 ■ Thimble Island Cruise: Stony Creek; 203 488 8905; Jun–mid-Oct; www.thimbleisland cruise.com

Stories and legends abound about the Thimble Islands, a cluster of diminutive islets located just off the coast. On a narrated scenic cruise you're very likely to hear a few of those tales, including the legend that the infamous pirate Captain Kidd buried treasure on Money Island. His gold hasn't been found to this day.

Islet, Thimble Islands

8 Boston Harbor Islands, MA

MAP F2 ■ 617 223 8666 ■ May–mid-Oct ■ www.bostonharborislands.org

The Boston Harbor Islands have sandy hiking and nature trails, lifeguard-protected beaches, and even a few old forts to explore. You can reach the islands by ferry from Boston's Long Wharf.

9 Martha's Vineyard, MA

MAP G5 ■ Steamship Authority: Woods Hole Terminal; 508 477 8600; www.islandferry.com

Martha's Vineyard has something for everyone, from proper Edgartown and the gingerbread architecture of Oak Bluffs to the sacred multicolored clay cliffs revered by the Aquinnah Wampanoag tribe.

Oak Bluffs, Martha's Vineyard

10 Burnt Island, ME

MAP P4 ■ Balmy Days Cruises: Pier 8, Boothbay Harbor; 207 633 2284; mid-Jul-Aug: 1:45pm Mon & Thu; adm; www.balmydayscruises.com

Cruise to this tiny island just outside Boothbay Harbor for a unique program illuminating the life of the lightkeeper and his family, who lived here around 1950.

TOP 10 LIGHTHOUSES

The Sheffield Island lighthouse

1 Sheffield Island
MAP B6 ■ Norwalk Harbor, CT
Handsome lighthouse built in 1868.

2 Stonington Harbor
MAP E5 ■ 7 Water St, Stonington, CT
Granite lighthouse, now a museum.

3 West Quoddy Head
MAP R2 ■ Quoddy Head State Park, Lubec, ME
This iconic candy-striped light (1857) marks the easternmost point of the US.

4 Marshall Point
MAP Q4 ■ Marshall Point Rd, Port Clyde, ME
Offshore light connected by a walkway to the keeper's house and museum.

5 Pemaquid Point
MAP P4 ■ Off Rte 130, Bristol, ME
Built high on these dramatic ledges in 1835, Pemaquid Point remains an essential navigational aid.

6 Portsmouth Harbor
MAP N6 ■ Off Rte 1B, New Castle, NH
Built in 1878, this is the latest of several built on New Castle island since 1771.

7 Beavertail
MAP E5 ■ Beavertail State Park, Jamestown, RI
This is the third-oldest light on the eastern seaboard, built in 1783.

8 Highland
MAP H3 ■ N Truro, MA
Set atop a bluff at the Cape Cod National Seashore, this is the highest light on the New England mainland.

9 Nobska Point
MAP G5 ■ Falmouth, MA
Sitting on the Shining Sea Bike Path, Nobska is visible for 16 miles (26 km).

10 Great Point
MAP H5 ■ Nantucket Island, MA
Rebuilt in 1986 as a historic replica in the Coskata-Coatue Wildlife Refuge.

🔟 Ocean Beaches

Brightly colored structures on the pier at Old Orchard Beach

1 Old Orchard Beach, Old Orchard, ME

Old Orchard has been a razzle-dazzle resort beach since trains first ran here in 1842. Three miles (5 km) of main beach guarantee plenty of room for sunbathing, swimming, kite-flying, and sandcastle-building. Shops, amusements, and rides ensure no one ever gets bored. During the summer there's a lively bar scene as well *(see p126)*.

2 Hampton Beach, Hampton, NH

MAP N6

Small, decorous state beaches dot Hampton's shoreline, but the main village beach is easily the most raucous, with outdoor concerts, sandcastle competitions, a flurry of summer activities, and a strip of souvenir shops and casual eateries. In summer the town is bilingual, reflecting its popularity with Quebec vacationers. Swimming is good, but the surf from offshore storms can make it challenging at times.

3 Crane Beach, Ipswich, MA

MAP G2 ■ Adm

This 7-mile (11-km) stretch of copious white sand is one of New England's most picturesque swimming beaches. Pack binoculars; Crane is legendary for its diversity of bird species, although some nesting grounds may be off-limits between May and early August.

4 Misquamicut State Beach, Westerly, RI

MAP E5 ■ Adm

Misquamicut (miss-KWAHM-i-cut) is one of New England's most popular family beaches, packing intense summer entertainment into a relatively short stretch of white sand. Most rides, amusement stands, and food kiosks open late June to August and some fall weekends, but the beach is accessible all year. Parking lots fill early on summer weekends.

5 Salty Brine State Beach, Narragansett, RI

MAP E5 ■ Adm

With solar-powered, hot-water showers and electricity from wind turbines to supply the juice to recharge electric vehicles, this is the "greenest" beach facility in New England. The narrow strip of fine golden sand at the entrance to Galilee harbor has gentle waves, great views of fishing vessels, and some of the coast's finest seafood.

6 Coast Guard Beach, Eastham, MA

MAP H4 ■ Adm

Arguably the best swimming beach on Cape Cod, Coast Guard Beach marks the beginning of the 30-mile (48 km) Great Beach of the Cape Cod National Seashore. A long and generous slope of sand leads down to the ocean, so the beach is never crowded. Stroll southward onto Nauset Spit to watch shore birds in summer, seals in winter.

7 Hammonasset Beach State Park, Madison, CT

MAP C5 ■ Adm ■ Camping late May–mid-Oct

More than 2 miles (3 km) of brown sand beaches lapped by the gentle waves of Long Island Sound lure summer swimmers and sunbathers in droves, but Connecticut's longest shorefront park also has an excellent nature center at Meigs Point. Fishermen stake out positions here early for excellent bluefish and striped bass fishing.

Vast sands at Hammonasset Beach

8 Old Silver Beach, Falmouth, MA

MAP G4 ■ Adm

This beautiful beach overlooking Buzzards Bay has warm summer waters, low waves, and a very gradual drop-off, making it an ideal swimming spot for young kids. Half the beach is reserved for Falmouth residents; the other half is open to all. Facing west over Buzzards Bay, Old Silver has some of New England's most spectacular sunsets.

Reid State Park coastline

9 Reid State Park, Georgetown, ME

MAP P4 ■ Adm

Reid State Park beaches are long strands of brown sand backed by high dunes – the antithesis of the "rocky coast of Maine." Mile Beach and Half Mile Beach have lifeguards, changing rooms, and snack bars in summer. You can swim safely along stretches sheltered from the ocean by sand bars, or break out the surf boards and head for more exposed parts of the beach.

10 Ogunquit Beach, Ogunquit, ME

MAP N5

A 2-mile (3-km) cove lined with brown sand, Ogunquit Beach is well served by a summer trolley system that makes parking a cinch. The south end of the beach terminates at romantic Marginal Way, a clifftop walking path through thickets of roses to the shops, restaurants, and copious art galleries of Perkins Cove.

TOP 10 Mountain Ski Areas

Skier on the slopes, Sunday River

1 Sunday River, Newry, ME

MAP M3 ▪ 15 South Ridge Rd ▪ 207 824 3000 ▪ Ski: mid-Nov–mid-Apr ▪ Adm ▪ www.sundayriver.com

The most accessible of Maine's high-mountain skiing, Sunday River splashes across eight interconnected peaks, with 135 diverse trails served by 15 lifts (including five high-speed quads). Lights extend evening skiing on most weekends and holidays. Snowmaking on 95 percent of terrain guarantees a long season. Evenings are enlived by the popular Shipyard Brew Haus microbrewery. During the summer it's a popular golf resort.

2 Bretton Woods, NH

MAP M3 ▪ 99 Ski Area Rd ▪ 603 378 3320 ▪ Ski: mid-Nov–Apr ▪ Adm ▪ www.brettonwoods.com

This is the largest ski area in New Hampshire boasting 464 acres (188 ha) of skiing and snowboarding on 62 trails, 35 glades, and three terrain parks. The ski area is closely allied with Omni Mount Washington Resort, so ski-stay packages give access to one of the last grand hotels of the White Mountains.

3 Killington, VT

MAP K5 ▪ 4763 Killington Rd ▪ 802 422 6200 ▪ Ski: mid-Nov–mid-Apr ▪ Adm ▪ www.killington.com

Killington Resort stretches across six mountain areas in central Vermont, providing 155 ski trails. As New England's largest ski resort, it also features 22 lifts, including two express gondolas and five express chairs, that give access to the highest lift-served ski terrain in the state of Vermont. Snowboarders' needs are also catered for with The Stash and Dream Maker terrain parks as well as the 500-ft (152-m) Superpipe with 22-ft (6.7-m) walls.

4 Mount Mansfield, Stowe, VT

MAP K3 ▪ 5781 Mountain Rd ▪ 802 253 3000 ▪ Ski: mid-Nov–mid-Apr ▪ Adm ▪ www.stowe.com

As the tallest of the attractive Green Mountains, Mansfield challenges hikers every summer and fall. Come winter, Stowe Mountain Resort takes over the slopes with 116 trails and more mile-long lifts than any other resort in the East. With average annual snowfall of 333 inches (8.46m), Stowe has a long season of deep snow. Summer golf resort.

5 Cannon Mountain, Franconia, NH

MAP L3 ▪ 9 Franconia Notch State Park ▪ 603 823 8800 ▪ Ski: Nov–mid-Apr ▪ Adm ▪ www.cannonmt.com

One of the oldest ski areas in the US, Cannon has a refreshingly non-commercial feel about it, not to mention the spectacular White Mountains vistas from its 98 trails.

A husky sledge ride, Bretton Woods

6 Attitash, Bartlett, NH

MAP M4 ▪ Rte 302 ▪ 800 223
7669 ▪ Ski: late Nov–Apr ▪ Adm
▪ www.attitash.com

Not as big or challenging as some
New England areas, Attitash (and
attached Bear Peak) have vistas of
the White Mountains to make the
skiing memorable. The longest
vertical drop is 1,750 ft (534 m),
but 11 lifts serve 70 trails.

Ski lift going up Sugarloaf

7 Sugarloaf, Carrabasset Valley, ME

MAP N2 ▪ 5092 Sugarloaf Access Rd
▪ 207 237 2000 ▪ Ski: mid-Nov–late
Apr ▪ Adm ▪ www.sugarloaf.com

Offering the only lift-served skiing
above the treeline in the East, its 54
miles (87 km) of trails crisscross
Sugarloaf, Maine's second-highest
peak at 4,237 ft (1,291 m). The
continuous vertical drop
of 2,820 ft (860 m) is New
England's longest. Sixty
of Sugarloaf's 162 trails
are rated difficult (black
diamond) or expert
(double black diamond).
Summer golf resort.

8 Smugglers' Notch, Jeffersonville, VT

MAP K3 ▪ 4323 Rte 108 S
▪ 802 644 8851 ▪ Ski: mid-
Nov–mid-Apr ▪ Adm
▪ www.smuggs.com

Smugglers' Notch, an
all-season family resort,
is well known for its

learn-to-ski programs and activities
for kids. The resort stretches across
three peaks, with 9 lifts serving 78
trails. The skiing at Smugglers' can
be challenging, despite its family
orientation; the Black Hole is the
only triple black diamond trail in the
Eastern US. Visit during the summer
and other attractions are offered as
well, including fishing, waterparks,
canoeing, and golf.

9 Mad River Glen, Waitsfield, VT

MAP K3 ▪ 802 496 3551 ▪ Ski:
mid-Dec–early Apr ▪ Adm
▪ www.madriverglen.com

This mountain, with some of the
East's most challenging terrain, is
run by a co-op of hardcore skiers
who keep it simple: no snowboards;
a single-chair lift from 1948 that
limits numbers on the slopes; and no
fancy lodge or hotels with hot tubs.

10 Stratton Mountain, Stratton, VT

MAP K6 ▪ 5 Village Lodge Rd ▪ 802
297 4000 ▪ Ski: Nov–early May ▪ Adm
▪ www.stratton.com

A pioneer in snowboarding, this
resort is located in the Green
Mountain National Forest near
Manchester, a town popular with
both skiers and shoppers. The 16
lifts serving 97 trails and top-ranked
terrain parks include four six-person
chair lifts. Summer golf resort.

🔟 Other Outdoor Activities and Sports

Hikers enjoying the scenery

① Hiking

Appalachian Trail: www.outdoors.org ■ Long Trail: www.greenmountainclub.org

Two US long-distance hiking trails cross New England. The Appalachian Trail begins in Georgia, crossing Vermont and New Hampshire before ending in Maine. The Long Trail traverses Vermont from south to north.

② Cross-Country Skiing

Trapp Family Lodge: MAP K3; 700 Trapp Hill Rd, Stowe, VT; 802 253 8511; www.trappfamily.com ■ Craftsbury Nordic Center: MAP K2; 535 Lost Nation Rd, Craftsbury Common, VT; 802 586 7767; open mid-Dec–Mar; adm; www.craftsbury.com

The epicenter of cross-country skiing is north-central Vermont. The Trapp family (of *Sound of Music* fame) introduced Nordic skiing in Stowe. Craftsbury Nordic Center is home to legendary cross-country ski races.

③ Schooner Sails

MAP Q3 ■ Rockland and Camden, ME ■ 800 807 WIND (9463) ■ Open Jun–Sep ■ Adm ■ www.sailmainecoast.com

Seals, porpoises, and whales are your neighbors as you sail where the winds take you with the schooners of Maine's windjammer fleet.

④ Bird-Watching

Wellfleet Bay: MAP H4; Rte 6, Wellfleet, MA; 508 349 2615; trails open 8am–dusk daily; adm; www.massaudubon.org ■ Audubon: MAP A6; 613 Riversville Rd, Greenwich, CT; 203 869 5272; open 9am–5pm daily; adm; greenwich.audubon.org

Observe shore birds plus warblers and other migratory species at Wellfleet Bay Wildlife Sanctuary on Cape Cod. The Audubon Society in Greenwich, Connecticut, runs a convivial annual count.

⑤ Golf

Samoset: MAP Q3; 220 Warrenton St, Rockport, ME; 207 594 2511; open May–Nov; adm; www.samosetresort.com ■ Ocean Edge: MAP H4; 2907 Main St, Brewster, MA; 508 896 9000; open Apr–Nov; adm; www.oceanedge.com

The most noted championship-level courses in New England include Samoset and Ocean Edge.

⑥ White-Water Rafting

MAP P1 ■ West Forks, ME ■ 800 723 8633 ■ Open May–early Oct ■ Adm ■ www.raftmaine.com

White-water rafting is hugely popular in Maine. Many trips depart from The Forks, a hamlet on the Kennebec.

Rafting on the Penobscot River

7 Bicycling
www.traillink.com

In Massachusetts, Minuteman Rail Trail cuts from Cambridge through Lexington and Concord. East Bay Bike Path is a tour of Narragansett Bay from Providence, Rhode Island. The Ashuelot Rail Trail from Keene to Hinsdale, New Hampshire, is a great way to explore covered bridges.

8 Whale-Watching
7 Seas: MAP G2; 63 Rogers St, Gloucester, MA; 888 283 1776; open late Apr–Oct; adm; www.7seas whalewatch.com

Large pods of whales summer on Stellwagen Bank. Take a cruise from Gloucester or Provincetown to look for finback, minke, and humpback whales, as well as dolphins.

Watching whales at Stellwagen Bank

9 Kayaking and Canoeing
Nauset: MAP H4; Goose Hummock Shops, Rte 6A, Orleans, MA; 508 255 2620; open May–Oct; adm; www.goose.com ▪ Allagash: MAP N3; Mahoosuc Guide Service, 1513 Bear River Rd, Newry, ME; 207 824 2073; open late May–Sep; adm; www.mahoosuc.com

Paddle among the wading birds of Nauset Marsh, or through Maine's pristine Allagash Wilderness.

10 Fishing
Orvis: MAP K6; 4180 Main St, Manchester, VT; 866 531 6213; www. orvis.com ▪ Frances Fleet: MAP E5; 33 State St, Narragansett, RI; 401 783 4988; adm; www.francesfleet.com

Orvis runs fly-fishing courses in Manchester, Vermont. Frances Fleet, operating out of Galilee, Rhode Island, offers deep-sea trips.

TOP 10 SPECTATOR SPORTS

Ice hockey player, Boston Bruins

1 Boston Red Sox
MAP S5 ▪ Fenway Park, Boston, MA ▪ Apr–Oct
Baseball's most hallowed park.

2 New England Patriots
MAP F3 ▪ Gillette Stadium, Foxborough, MA ▪ Sep–Jan
The Patriots are perennial Super Bowl contenders.

3 Boston Celtics
MAP W2 ▪ TD Garden, above North Station, Boston, MA ▪ Oct–May
Hoop dreams ramp up each fall as the Celtics take the court.

4 Boston Bruins
MAP W2 ▪ TD Garden, above North Station, Boston, MA ▪ Oct–Apr
One of the founding teams of the National Hockey League.

5 Head of the Charles Regatta
MAP F2 ▪ mid-Oct
The world's largest two-day rowing event between Cambridge and Boston.

6 Boston Marathon
MAP F2 ▪ mid-Apr
The world's oldest annual marathon, from Hopkinton to Boston.

7 New Hampshire Motor Speedway
MAP M5 ▪ Loudon, NH ▪ Apr–Oct
Sports cars, stock cars, and even go-karts thrill fans with their speed.

8 Newport Regatta
Topsail racing in the home of American yachting (see p19).

9 US National Toboggan Championships
MAP Q3 ▪ Camden, ME ▪ Feb
Open-entry field of contestants at the Camden Snow Bowl.

10 New England Revolution
MAP F3 ▪ Gillette Stadium, Foxborough, MA ▪ Mar–Dec
Boston's professional soccer team.

Following pages Covered bridge in Franconia, New Hampshire

PEMIGEWASSET RIVER
1886

MAX LOAD IS TONS

Ways to See Foliage

① Green Mountain Railroad, VT
MAP K5 ■ 535 Depot St, Chester ■ 802 463 3069 ■ Open Jul–mid-Oct ■ Adm ■ www.rails-vt.com

Take a jaunt through the southern Vermont woods aboard vintage rail-cars, which are pulled by a diesel locomotive, for some spectacular views of the Connecticut River and the deep gorges of its tributaries. In fall, the maple trees are a dazzling blaze of flame-like colors.

② Mohawk Trail, MA
This historic Indian trade route over the Berkshire Hills follows the upper ranges of the Deerfield River – resplendent with acid-yellow alder and birch – until it climbs through fiery stands of maple, birch, and beech in the Charlemont State Forest. The drive ends by spiraling down the hillsides at the aptly named Hairpin Turn (see p80).

Colorful forests at Lake Champlain

③ Lake Champlain Cruise, VT
MAP J3 ■ Burlington Boathouse, 1 College St, Burlington ■ 802 862 8300 ■ Open mid-May–mid-Oct ■ Adm ■ www.soea.com

Hop aboard the *Spirit of Ethan Allen III* for a narrated cruise around Lake Champlain. While adults admire the brightly painted forests that surround the lake, kids ought to keep an eye out for Champ, the legendary sea serpent that resides in the lake.

④ K-1 Gondola, VT
After a scenic gondola ride to the highest lift-served terrain in Vermont, a short, easy hike brings you to the summit of Killington Peak (see p54) for a panoramic view of five states and part of Canada.

Fall foliage, Kancamagus Highway

⑤ Kancamagus Highway, NH
Few foliage drives in New England match the thrill of hurtling along the "Kanc" through a tunnel of kaleido-scopic colors. This stretch of highway runs between Lincoln and Conway and covers about 34 miles (55 km) of Route 112. Stop along the way to savor the experience by hiking to a waterfall or sunning on mid-stream glacial boulders (see p20).

⑥ Essex Steam Train and Riverboat, CT
Combine a trip through the woods in restored 1920s railcars pulled by coal-fired steam locomotives with a cruise down the Connecticut River aboard a three-deck Mississippi-style riverboat (see p99).

⑦ Route 100, VT
MAP K2–6
Perhaps New England's ultimate road for leaf-peeping, Route 100 passes natural wonders like Moss Glen Falls, follows the Mad River through several scenic villages, then rises high into the Green Mountains.

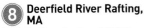

8 Deerfield River Rafting, MA

MAP C2 ▪ Zoar Outdoor: 800 532 7483; open Jun–Sep; adm; www.zoaroutdoor.com

The Deerfield River has some of the most exhilarating rapids and most scenic gorges in New England. Nothing compares to the rush of bankside colors viewed from a raft during foliage season.

9 Boston's Emerald Necklace

MAP V4–W4 ▪ www.emeraldnecklace.org

Boston is blessed with an almost continuous chain of parks stretching from downtown skyscrapers to leafy suburbia. This walking and cycle route begins at Boston Common. In the fall, the parks are an explosion of red, purple, orange, and yellow.

10 Mount Monadnock, NH

MAP L6 ▪ Off Rte 124, west of Jaffrey ▪ 603 532 8862 ▪ Open sunrise–sunset daily ▪ Adm ▪ www.nhstateparks.org

The 3,165-ft (965-m) summit of Mount Monadnock offers incredible views. The scramble over boulders is well worth the effort, especially during colorful fall foliage season.

Hiker at Mount Monadnock

TOP 10 COVERED BRIDGES

Charming covered Stark Bridge

1 Bulls Bridge, 1842
MAP B4 ▪ Rte 7, Kent, CT
Town lattice and queenspost over the Housatonic River.

2 Cornish-Windsor Bridge, 1866
MAP L5 ▪ Rte 12A, Plainfield, NH
Town lattice, rebuilt in 1989. Spans the Connecticut River between New Hampshire and Vermont.

3 Hemlock Bridge, 1857
MAP M4 ▪ Off Rte 302, Fryeburg, ME
Paddleford truss over the Saco River.

4 Artist's Covered Bridge, 1872
MAP N3 ▪ Off Rtes 2 and 26, Newry, ME
Paddleford truss, also known as the Sunday River Bridge.

5 Stark Bridge, 1862
MAP M3 ▪ North Rd, Stark, NH
Paddleford truss spanning the Upper Ammonoosuc River in the village.

6 Albany Covered Bridge, 1858
MAP M4 ▪ Dugway Rd, off the Kancamagus Hwy, Albany, NH
Altered Paddleford truss across the Swift River.

7 Ashuelot Bridge, 1864
MAP K6 ▪ South of Rte 119, Bolton Rd, Upper Village, Winchester, NH
Town lattice truss that spans the Ashuelot River.

8 Warren Bridge, 1880
MAP K4 ▪ East of Rte 100, Warren, VT
Asymmetrical queenspost stretching across the Mad River.

9 Paper Mill, Silk, and Henry Bridges, 1840–2000
MAP J6 ▪ South of Rte 67A, Bennington, VT
Three bridges on the Waloomsac River.

10 Burkeville Bridge, 1870
MAP C2 ▪ Rte 116, Conway, MA
Howe truss bridge stretching across the South River.

Children's Attractions

geodesic dome. Life-size dioramas re-create scenes from the Jurassic and Triassic eras.

Riding a zipline, Ramblewild

(1) Ramblewild, Lanesborough, MA
MAP B2 ■ 110 Brodie Mountain Rd ■ 844 472 6253 ■ Open Nov–Apr: 11am–1pm Fri–Sun; May–Oct: 10am–3pm daily ■ Adm ■ www.ramblewild.com

Eight trails of varying difficulty snake through the canopy with logs, nets, ziplines, rope bridges, and more.

(2) Boston Children's Museum
MAP X4 ■ 308 Congress St ■ 617 426 6500 ■ Open 10am–5pm Sat–Thu (to 9pm Fri) ■ Adm ■ www.bostonkids.org

Hands-on learning fills two former wool warehouses. Children can scale a climbing sculpture, explore the magic of soap bubbles, or join in short plays and shows on KidStage.

(3) Dinosaur State Park, Rocky Hill, CT
MAP C4 ■ 400 West St ■ 860 529 8423 ■ Open 9am–4:30pm Tue–Sun ■ Adm ■ www.dinosaurstatepark.org

Children are awestruck by more than 500 dinosaur fossil tracks preserved beneath a

(4) McAuliffe-Shepard Discovery Center, Concord, NH
MAP M5 ■ 2 Institute Dr ■ 603 271 7827 ■ Open mid-Jun–early Sep: 10:30am–4pm daily (Fri–Sat in off-season) ■ Adm ■ www.starhop.com

Kids are encouraged to reach for the stars at this space exploration center named for astronauts Alan B. Shepard and Christa McAuliffe.

(5) Six Flags New England, Agawam, MA
MAP C3 ■ Rte 159 ■ 413 786 9300 ■ Open Apr–Oct, call for hours ■ Adm ■ www.sixflags.com

Some of the fastest, tallest, wildest, and most gut-wrenching thrill rides in the country await at this Six Flags amusement park located beside the Connecticut River.

(6) Roger Williams Park and Zoo, Providence, RI
MAP E4 ■ 1000 Elmwood Ave ■ 401 785 3510 ■ Open 9am–5pm daily (Oct–Mar: to 4pm) ■ Adm ■ www.rwpzoo.org

Visitors can ride the carousel or enjoy a boat ride on the lake in this sprawling park, but save time for the zoo – one of the best in the country, placed in a naturalistic setting. The zoo is laid out in themed areas where you can come face to face with over 100 species.

Elephant, Roger Williams Zoo

7 Basketball Hall of Fame, Springfield, MA

MAP C3 ■ 1000 Hall of Fame Ave ■ 413 781 6500 or 877 4HOOPLA ■ Open 10am–4pm Tue–Fri, Sun, 10am–5pm Sat ■ Adm ■ www.hoophall.com

This complex in the birthplace of basketball celebrates the sport with footage of games, star players' memorabilia, and interactive exhibits that are suitable for kids.

8 Lake Compounce, Bristol, CT

MAP C4 ■ 186 Enterprise Dr ■ 860 583 3300 ■ Open May–Oct, call for schedule ■ Adm ■ www.lakecompounce.com

A 1911 carousel, a 1927 roller coaster, and an antique trolley maintain the ambience of an old-fashioned amusement park.

Penguins, New England Aquarium

9 New England Aquarium, Boston

MAP X3 ■ Central Wharf ■ 617 973 5200 ■ Open Jul–Aug: 9am–6pm Sun–Thu, 9am–7pm Fri–Sat; Sep–Jun: 9am–5pm Mon–Fri, 9am–6pm Sat–Sun ■ Adm ■ www.neaq.org

Kids love the acrobatics of the harbor seals, the antics of more than 80 penguins, and the shark and ray tank.

10 Ben & Jerry's Ice Cream Factory, Waterbury, VT

Ben Cohen and Jerry Greenfield said business should not be dull, and the factory tour of Ben & Jerry's is a real hoot. The goal is the tasting room at the end, where you might sample flavors in development (see p111).

TOP 10 CAROUSELS

The carousel at Bushnell Park

1 Flying Horse Carousel
MAP E5 ■ Bay St, Watch Hill, RI ■ Adm
Beachfront carousel that is one of the oldest in New England.

2 Fall River Carousel
MAP F4 ■ Battleship Cove, Fall River, MA ■ Adm
Built by the Philadelphia Toboggan Company in 1920.

3 Shelburne Museum
A vintage 1920s carousel that operates right outside the Shelburne Museum's Circus Building (see p41).

4 Crescent Park Carousel
MAP F4 ■ 700 Bullocks Point Ave, East Providence, RI ■ Adm
Charles I.D. Looff showcase.

5 Bushnell Park Carousel
MAP C4 ■ Bushnell Park, Hartford, CT ■ Adm
Beautiful three-row hand-carved wooden carousel.

6 Flying Horses Carousel
MAP G5 ■ Oak Bluffs Ave, Oak Bluffs, Martha's Vineyard, MA ■ Adm
1876–8 CWF Dare Company model.

7 Slater Memorial Park
MAP E4 ■ Pawtucket, RI ■ Adm
This 1895 carousel includes a camel, a giraffe, a lion, and two chariots.

8 Story Land
MAP M4 ■ Rte 16, Glen, NH ■ Adm
A strikingly unusual early 20th-century German carousel.

9 Heritage State Park
MAP C3 ■ 221 Appleton St, Holyoke, MA ■ Adm
This 1929 carousel has 20 standing horses and 28 jumpers.

10 Lighthouse Point Park
MAP C5 ■ 2 Lighthouse Point Rd, New Haven, CT ■ Adm
A 1916 carousel with 72 original figures.

🔟 New England Foods

1 Clams

It's easy to get confused by New England clams. "Quahog" is the Native-American name for the hard-shelled clam *Mercenaria mercenaria*, but the bivalve has other aliases. Small ones, known as "littlenecks," are served as the ever-popular battered-and-fried clam. Medium-sized quahogs are known as "cherrystones," and are often eaten raw. Big ones are stuffed and baked.

2 Maple Syrup

Nothing tames a Yankee sourpuss like pouring on the maple syrup over a stack of pancakes or waffles. In late winter, you might encounter sugar houses in the north of New England boiling down the sap of sugar maple trees. Stop for a jug – you'll never find it cheaper.

3 Scallops

Scallops were popular in New England cooking long before they

Maple syrup

became a mainstay of gourmet restaurants. Look for them sautéed in butter, breaded and deep-fried, or tossed with linguine, herbs, and olive oil. Scallops are on almost every menu, not least because New Bedford, Massachusetts, lands more scallops than any other port in the world.

4 Cranberries

Popular in juices and muffins, cranberries are best known for the sugary sauce served as part of traditional Thanksgiving dinner. The state of Massachusetts still produces about half of America's cranberry crop.

Fresh New England lobsters

5 Lobster

One of the pleasures of a New England summer is setting a steamed lobster on a picnic table, cracking it with a rock, and savoring the sweet meat with melted butter. *Homarus americanus*, often called "Maine lobster," is the world's largest crustacean, and is generally served at weights of 1¼–3 lb (0.5–1.3 kg).

6 Oysters

New England oysters are found on sandy bottoms all along the coast, but those cultured in beds near Damariscotta, Maine; Wellfleet, Massachusetts; and Norwalk, Connecticut, are celebrated for their delicate, distinctive flavors.

Oysters served on the half shell

7 Cheese

Visitors will find world-class farmstead cheeses all across New England. Small dairies make everything from fresh goat's milk chevre to aged, pungent blues. Somewhat larger Vermont cheese companies also produce superb American cheddar and Colby cheeses.

8 Blueberries

Whether you prefer the light blueberry accent of a muffin or the supreme intensity of a blueberry pie, there's no substitute for the tiny "wild" lowbush blueberry. Most wild blueberries are harvested in Maine from late July through August, but they freeze well, so blueberry baked treats are available all year.

Tray of blueberry muffins

9 Stone-ground Cornmeal

Order a jonnycake – a sweet cornmeal pancake cooked on a griddle – at any Rhode Island diner, and you'll be enjoying a culinary tradition going back to the region's first European colonists and the Native Americans before them.

10 Heirloom Apples

Look for orchard farmstands selling apples in the fall. Many historic apple varieties can be traced to their New England birthplace by name (Roxbury Russet, Westfield-Seek-No-Further). Preservation efforts begun in the 1980s have borne fruit in the widespread availability of dozens of historic varieties.

TOP 10 DRINKS

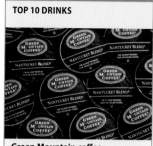

Green Mountain coffee

1 Moxie
Invented in 1876 by medical doctor Augustin Thompson, this soft drink with an appropriately medicinal aftertaste is now the official beverage of the state of Maine.

2 Apple Cider
Freshly pressed and unfiltered apple juice is widely available in the fall.

3 Sam Adams Lager
The flagship brew of the Boston Beer Company launched the national craft beer revolution.

4 Del's Lemonade
A thirst-quenching Rhode Island favorite, this contains only lemon juice, sugar, and shaved ice.

5 Poland Spring Water
This brand of bottled water originating in a former Maine spa town is now distributed widely in New England.

6 Coffee Milk
Rhode Island's official state drink is created by stirring coffee syrup into milk.

7 Sparkling Wines from Westport Rivers Winery
Estate-grown chardonnay and pinot noir grapes are used to make New England's best bubbly.

8 Green Mountain Coffee
The gourmet coffee roaster's blends are sold throughout the region.

9 Lincoln Peak Vineyards Marquette
The signature red wine of this Vermont winery demonstrates the triumph of artful winemaking over harsh climate.

10 Frappe
Pronounced "frap," this thick milkshake includes ice cream and syrup in true New England style.

Restaurants

1 Fore Street, Portland, ME

A handsome, exposed-brick dining room always filled with foodies. Wood-burning fires in the open kitchen cook and flavor fresh seafood and meats. Raw materials come from a community of Maine farmers, fishermen, foragers, and cheese-makers *(see p129)*.

2 Menton, Boston, MA

This temple of French-Italian haute cuisine in the Boston Seaport is the flagship of chef-owner Barbara Lynch's culinary empire. Menton is noted for Lynch's imaginative seafood (including shrimp with chicory, almond, and horseradish), perfect service, and brilliant wine pairings *(see p83)*.

Foie gras with chestnuts, Menton

3 Ristorante Massimo, Portsmouth, NH

New England seafood acquires an Italian accent here, in this sophisticated dining room in a historic waterfront building. Don't miss the yellowfin tuna and lobster with lemon risotto *(see p121)*.

4 Stars, Chatham, MA

MAP H4 ▪ Chatham Bars Inn, 297 Shore Rd ▪ 508 945 0096 ▪ Hours vary with season ▪ $$$

Perhaps the most elegant special-occasion dining on Cape Cod, Stars emphasizes the bounty of the inn's own farm, the catch landed just feet away at Chatham Fish Pier, and superb dry-aged beef.

Exterior of Craigie On Main

5 Craigie On Main, MA

Chef Tony Maws, who is nationally acclaimed for his French-inspired nose-to-tail approach to fine dining, presides over a bustling open kitchen facing the dining area filled with an eclectic mix of diners. Head to the bar for its wildly popular gourmet burger *(see p83)*.

6 Inn at Shelburne Farms Restaurant, VT

Inn guests always admire the Shelburne Farms market garden, and the food tastes as good as it looks. Produce that is sourced directly from this and other local farms is used to create a wonderful seasonal menu of classic Continental dishes with an American accent. Meals are served either in the elegant marble dining room or on the outdoor terrace *(see p113)*.

The restaurant at Shelburne Farms

⑦ Primo Restaurant, Rockland, ME

Freshness is key at this intimate coastal restaurant. The innovative menu depends on produce just pulled from the ground as well as local fish just pulled from the sea. The chef-owner raises her own produce and makes the sausages from her own pigs *(see p129)*.

⑧ Al Forno, Providence, RI

A wood-fired oven provides the searing heat essential for cooking spectacular Northern Italian meat dishes like chorizo-stuffed quails with plum jam, as well as Al Forno's signature baked pasta dishes. The style is Italian; most ingredients are local *(see p91)*.

Tables at the Union League Café

⑨ Union League Café, New Haven, CT

New England meat, produce, and spectacular fish get the French brasserie treatment at this classy but cozy dining spot at the edge of Yale University. There's also an outstanding raw bar of New England shellfish *(see p100)*.

⑩ Old Inn on the Green, New Marlborough, MA

MAP B3 ▪ 134 Hartsville–New Marlboro Rd ▪ 413 229 7924 ▪ Closed L, Mon & Tue Nov–Jun ▪ $$

Genuinely antique, the inn has no electricity, so candles light the tables and fireplaces glow in season. There is nothing old-fashioned about the contemporary farm-to-table menus.

TOP 10 PLACES TO EAT SEAFOOD

Abbott's Lobster in the Rough

1 Five Islands Lobster Co
MAP P4 ▪ 207 371 2990 ▪ 1447 Five Islands Rd, Georgetown, ME
Georgetown pier lobster shack.

2 Woodman's of Essex
MAP G2 ▪ 978 768 6057 ▪ 121 Main St, Essex, MA
Their fried clams are among the best.

3 Evelyn's Drive-In
MAP F4 ▪ 401 624 3100 ▪ 2335 Main Rd, Tiverton, RI
Famous for their stuffed clams.

4 Barking Crab
MAP X4 ▪ 617 426 CRAB ▪ 88 Sleeper St, Boston, MA
Clam-shack ambience comes to the Boston waterfront.

5 Abbott's Lobster in the Rough
MAP D5 ▪ 860 536 7719 ▪ 117 Pearl St, Noank, CT
Butter-drenched lobster meat in a bun.

6 Shaw's Fish & Lobster Wharf
Diners can watch lobster boats come and go in the narrow inlet *(see p128)*.

7 George's of Galilee
MAP E5 ▪ 401 783 2306 ▪ 250 Sand Hill Cove Rd, Galilee, RI
George's has had pick of the catch since 1948.

8 Net Result
MAP G5 ▪ 508 693 6071 ▪ 79 Beach Rd, Vineyard Haven, MA
Perfect fish. The menu varies with the catch of the day.

9 Lenny & Joe's Fish Tale
MAP D5 ▪ 860 669 0767 ▪ Rte 1, Westbrook, CT
Clear clam chowder with a hint of milk.

10 Bookstore Restaurant
MAP H4 ▪ 508 349 3154 ▪ 50 Kendrick Ave, Wellfleet, MA
Oysters don't come any fresher.

For key to restaurant price ranges see p83

TOP 10 Shopping Destinations

Brimfield antiques flea market

1 Brimfield, MA
MAP D3 ▪ May, Jul, Sep
▪ www.brimfieldshows.com
Whether you're seeking Art Deco jewelry or furniture crafted in Salem in the 1790s, Brimfield is the place to look. Antiques hunters from around the world converge on this small town for its three annual antiques shows in May, July, and September.

2 League of New Hampshire Craftsmen Fair, NH
MAP L5 ▪ Mount Sunapee Resort, Newbury, NH ▪ Early Aug ▪ Adm
▪ www.nhcrafts.org
Established in 1933, the League of New Hampshire Craftsmen Fair is the oldest craft fair in the US. More than 200 juried members of the League offer their work, including jewelry, fine furniture, pottery, glass blowing, and weaving.

3 Woodbury, CT
MAP B5 ▪ www.antiqueswoodbury.com
Dealers in fine US and British antiques set up shop here around half a century ago. They've since been joined by dealers in import porcelain, Oriental rugs, and whatever is giving New York interior decorators shivers this season.

4 Shoppes at Buckland Hills, Manchester, CT
MAP C4 ▪ 194 Buckland Hills Dr
▪ www.theshoppesatbucklandhills.com
Central Connecticut's largest shopping area, this features virtually every big-box national chain store, including discount electronics, decor, and home goods dealers like the Christmas Tree Shop.

5 Providence Place, Providence, RI
MAP E4 ▪ One Providence Pl
▪ www.providenceplace.com
This mega-mall in downtown Providence has captured most of the retail activity in Rhode Island's capital. Stores occupy three levels, with entertainment and a food court above the shops.

6 Freeport, ME
MAP P4 ▪ www.freeportusa.com
Outdoors outfitter L. L. Bean set the tone here when it opened in 1911. Freeport has since blossomed as a world-famous shopper's paradise; more than 170 shops offer the biggest and best name brands in American merchandising – often at substantial discounts.

The L. L. Bean store in Freeport

7 Manchester, VT
MAP K6 ■ www.
manchesterdesigneroutlets.com

Three dozen or so designer outlets with top fashion names like Armani, Tse, and Michael Kors, and home decor ranging from silver tableware to hand-woven Tibetan rugs, make Manchester, Vermont, a mecca for picking up upscale bargains.

8 Harvard Square, Cambridge, MA
MAP F2 ■ www.harvardsquare.com

America's most literary city is home to two comprehensive bookstores, one of which prints out-of-print titles on demand. Also around Harvard Square are specialists in used books, poetry, foreign and Marxist literature, and comic books.

Searching for books, Harvard Square

9 Weston, VT
General stores face each other across the main street in this picturesque village. The warren of rooms in the Vermont Country Store contains all kinds of clever gadgets, outdoors apparel, cooking utensils, and an excellent selection of New England foods (see p111).

10 Wellfleet Flea Market & Drive-In, Wellfleet, MA
MAP H4 ■ Rte 6 ■ Apr–Oct ■ Adm ■ www.wellfleetcinemas.com/flea-market

More than 200 vendors offer a mixture of trash and treasures, including the occasional antique, in the wide-open spaces of a drive-in theater near the end of Cape Cod.

TOP 10 SOUVENIRS

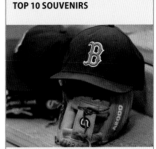

Red Sox baseball cap

1 Vermont Snow Globe
Capture winter permanently to set on your knickknack shelf.

2 Tom Brady Bobblehead Doll
The quarterback of the New England Patriots football team is gridiron hero to some, matinee idol to others.

3 Black Dog T-shirt
A black labrador T-shirt says "Martha's Vineyard" to anyone who has ever visited the Black Dog restaurant there.

4 Red Sox Baseball Cap
Show your loyalty in the epic rivalry between the Boston Red Sox and the New York Yankees.

5 Lobster Keychain
The bright crimson of New England's quintessential crustacean makes your keys easier to spot.

6 Pine-Scented Pillow
Mainers have been selling these fragrant headrests to tourists since steamships first started running in the 1830s.

7 "This Car Climbed Mount Washington" Bumper Sticker
People will regard your old clunker with new respect.

8 Nantucket Lightship Basket
True folk art commands high prices for basket-purses with fashion cachet.

9 Woody Jackson "Holy Cow" Art
Jackson's cow-themed art has cornered the market on the iconic black-and-white Vermont cows, with prints, cards, calendars, collectibles, and T-shirts.

10 Maine Tourmaline Jewelry
The most famous Western Maine tourmalines are "watermelon" stones with pink centers and green edges.

New England for Free

1 Free Fun Fridays, MA
www.highlandstreet
foundation.org/freefunfridays.html
Admission to eight different
museums or cultural attractions
throughout Massachusetts is free
each Friday from late June through
August. See the website for institutions that take part.

2 National Park Service Freedom Trail Walking Tours, MA
MAP W3 ■ National Park
Service Downtown Visitor
Center, Faneuil Hall, 1
Faneuil Hall Sq, Boston ■ 617
242 5642 ■ Call for hours
■ www.nps.gov/bost
Park Rangers offer two
free walking tours of
Boston's Freedom Trail –
from Faneuil Hall to Old
South Meeting House
and from Faneuil Hall
to Old North Church.

3 Yale University Art Museums, New Haven, CT
The Yale University Art Gallery and
the Yale Center for British Art have
spectacular collections in landmark
Louis B. Kahn buildings from early
and late in his career (see p42).

Town crier actor on Freedom Trail tour

4 Green Mountain Trails, VT
MAP K3 ■ Green Mountain Club, 4711
Waterbury-Stowe Rd ■ 802 244 7037
■ Open 9am–5pm daily (mid-Oct–
mid-May: Mon–Fri)
■ www.greenmountainclub.org
Green Mountain Club's visitor center
provides information, current trail
conditions, and maps for hiking
mountain trails all over Vermont.

5 Project Puffin Visitor Center, ME
MAP Q3 ■ 311 Main St,
Rockland ■ 207 596
5566 ■ Open May:
10am–5pm Wed–Sun;
Jun–Oct: 10am–5pm
daily ■ www.project
puffin.audubon.org
At the Project Puffin Visitor
Center tourists can learn about
the ongoing seabird restoration
programs on Maine's offshore
islands and experience live
video and audio feeds of
puffin rookeries – one of
the great bird conserva-
tion success stories.

6 Cliffwalk, RI
MAP F5 ■ Memorial Drive to
Ochre Point, Newport ■ 401 845 5300
■ www.cliffwalk.com
This 3.5-mile (5.5-km) walk above the
natural rocky shore skirts
the backyards of some of
Newport's most dramatic
Gilded Age mansions.
Parts of the southern half
are on a rough trail.

7 Hampton Beach Concerts and Fireworks, NH
MAP N6 ■ 115 Ocean
Blvd, Hampton Beach
■ www.hamptonbeach.
org ■ Jun–Aug
Every night throughout
the summer free con-
certs of various music

Indo-Pacific galleries, Yale Art Gallery

genres are held on Hampton Beach, capped off each Wednesday with a display of fireworks at 9:30pm.

8 UConn Dairy Barn Tours, CT

MAP D4 ■ Horsebarn Hill Rd, Storrs ■ 860 486 2634 ■ Open 10am–4pm daily ■ www.animalscience.uconn.edu

Visit the University of Connecticut dairy herd and watch the afternoon milking. Ice cream from their milk is sold at the adjacent Dairy Bar.

Budweiser Brewery Experience

9 Budweiser Brewery Experience, NH

Opened in 1970, the Merrimack site nestled in beautiful countryside is the company's largest New England brewery. The complimentary tour traces the process of making Budweiser beer "from seed to sip," and over 21s have the opportunity to sample some of the products at the end. Visitors also get the chance to meet the world-famous Budweiser Clydesdale horses (see p118).

10 WaterFire, Providence, RI

Braziers floating on canals create a magical aura around the Providence waterfront for concerts and citywide celebration. Check the website for the schedule of events (see p72).

TOP 10 MONEY-SAVING TIPS

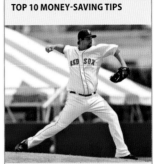

Red Sox team member

1 In Boston, BosTix booths at Copley Square and Faneuil Hall sell discounted theater, music, dance, and comedy tickets. www.artsboston.org.bostix

2 The Red Sox farm-team games in Pawtucket, RI cost much less than a game at Fenway. www.pawsox.com

3 MBTA weekly passes offer big savings on subway and bus fares in and around Boston. www.mbta.com

4 Many museums and hotels offer discounts to seniors, students, or members of AAA.

5 Most museums offer a period of free admission each week. Check their websites for details.

6 Purchase fuel from Tuesday to Thursday for the week's lowest prices.

7 Purchase cheap lunches or picnic ingredients at farmers' markets.

8 The America the Beautiful Pass covers admission and fees at more than 2,000 federal recreation sites. www.nps.gov/findapark/passes.htm

9 The $3 Cabot Cheese Factory Tour in Cabot, VT, includes free samples.

10 Eat an affordable lunch instead of dinner at one of New England's top restaurants.

Farmers' market apples

Events

1 Winter Carnival, Stowe, VT

MAP K3 ▪ Stowe, VT ▪ 802 253 7321 ▪ late Jan ▪ www.stowewinter carnival.com

Plummeting temperatures and falling snow are celebrated with snow golf, snow volleyball, and ice-carving.

2 Patriot's Day

MAP E2 ▪ Lexington and Concord, MA ▪ 978 369 6993 ▪ 3rd Mon in Apr ▪ www.nps.gov/mima

This re-enactment of the opening salvos of the American Revolution starts before dawn in Lexington and continues on to nearby Concord.

3 WaterFire, Providence, RI

MAP E4 ▪ Providence, RI ▪ 401 273 1155 ▪ May–Nov ▪ Donation ▪ www.waterfire.org

Nothing epitomizes the renaissance of the Providence waterfront as well as WaterFire, an environmental sculpture by Barnaby Evans. Its 80 floating bonfires, on the city's three downtown rivers, make a magical setting for a host of summer arts events.

4 Jazz and Folk Festivals, Newport, RI

MAP F5 ▪ Newport, RI ▪ Summer ▪ Adm ▪ newportjazzfest.org; www.newportfolk.org

For over 50 years, these festivals have been a focus for fresh talent as well as for star performers. Fort Adams State Park, set at the mouth of the harbor with panoramic views of Newport Bridge and the East Passage, makes a perfect venue.

5 International Festival of Arts & Ideas, New Haven, CT

MAP C5 ▪ New Haven, CT ▪ 888 278 4332 ▪ mid-Jun ▪ www.artidea.org

Every June, New Haven holds hundreds of events, the majority free, including opera on New Haven Green, hip-hop poets, dance, and readings by Nobel Laureate authors.

6 Windjammer Days, Boothbay Harbor, ME

MAP P4 ▪ Boothbay Harbor, ME ▪ 207 633 2353 ▪ late Jun ▪ www.windjammerdays.org

Two days of family fun include windjammer cruise schooners and other tall ships in Boothbay Harbor, an antique boat parade, waterfront concerts, a craft fair, and fireworks.

7 Independence Day Celebrations

Bristol, RI: MAP F4; www.july4th bristolri.com ▪ Boston, MA: MAP F2; www.july4th.org

The red-white-and-blue stripe marks the Fourth of July parade route in Bristol, Rhode Island, site of one of the nation's most enthusiastic

Chick Corea, Newport Jazz Festival

small-town parades. The televised Independence Day celebration in Boston is famous nationwide for its fireworks and Boston Pops concert.

⑧ Green River Festival, Greenfield, MA

MAP C2 ▪ Greenfield Community College, College Dr ▪ mid-Jul ▪ Adm ▪ www.greenriverfestival.com

The festival is a combination of hot-air ballooning and music, featuring folk, Americana, bluegrass, indie rock, Cajun, and zydeco music in a fairground venue. On-site camping pitches are available.

Hot-air balloons, Green River Festival

⑨ Maine Lobster Festival

MAP Q3 ▪ Rockland, ME ▪ 207 596 0376 ▪ late Jul–early Aug ▪ Adm ▪ www.mainelobsterfestival.com

More than 20,000 lb (9,000 kg) of lobster are steamed every year for this Rockland waterfront festival. Lobstermen race across floating crates, floats parade down the street, and a beauty contest chooses a Sea Goddess to preside over the event.

⑩ Thanksgiving Celebration, Plymouth, MA

MAP G3 ▪ Plymouth, MA ▪ 508 747 7525 ▪ 4th Thu in Nov ▪ www.seeplymouth.com

Descendants of *Mayflower* pilgrims re-enact the Thanksgiving celebration of 1621. Another ceremony highlights original Native American culture.

TOP 10 AGRICULTURAL FAIRS

Fairgoers at Woodstock

1 Barnstable County Fair
MAP G5 ▪ Rte 151, E Falmouth, MA ▪ mid-Jul
Demolition derby and bull-riding top the entertainment here.

2 Cheshire Fair
MAP L6 ▪ 247 Monadnock Hwy, Swanzey, NH ▪ late Jul–early Aug
Pony pulls, puppets, pie-eating, and country music.

3 Addison County Fair & Field Days
MAP J4 ▪ 1790 Field Days Rd, New Haven, VT ▪ early Aug
Vermont's largest agricultural fair.

4 Washington County Fair
MAP E5 ▪ Rte 112, Richmond, RI ▪ mid–late Aug
Don't miss the rooster-crowing contest.

5 Brooklyn Fair
MAP D4 ▪ Rte 169, Brooklyn, CT ▪ late Aug
Nashville entertainment, old-fashioned midway rides, and prize poultry.

6 Woodstock Fair
MAP D4 ▪ South Woodstock, CT ▪ late Aug–early Sep
Long-established harvest celebration and rural home-coming.

7 Champlain Valley Fair
MAP J3 ▪ Essex Junction, VT ▪ late Aug–early Sep
From extreme motorcycle show to sheep and dairy exhibits.

8 Eastern States Exposition
MAP C3 ▪ 1305 Memorial Ave, West Springfield, MA ▪ mid-Sep–Oct
New England's largest fair.

9 Fryeburg Fair
MAP M4 ▪ Fryeburg, ME ▪ early Oct
This traditional agricultural fair also features woodsmen competitions.

10 Topsfield Fair
MAP F2 ▪ Topsfield, MA ▪ early Oct
Farmers have gathered here since 1818.

New England
Area by Area

Lighthouse at Portland Head, Maine

TOP10 Massachusetts

Massachusetts is where English settlers first imagined remaking their homeland in a wilderness they called New England. For all

their Englishness, they named the bay between Cape Cod and the mainland after the coastal Massachusett tribe, then took the bay's name for their colony. The towns of Plymouth, Salem, and Boston were the beachhead from which the rest of New England was colonized. As the state with the first college, first democratic government, first rebels to defy the king, first authors to invent an American literature, and the first sailors to open the ports of Asia to the West, Massachusetts claims that much of what matters about New England happened here first. The state remains a pioneer of science and culture to this day.

Whaling Museum, Nantucket

AREA MAP OF MASSACHUSETTS

Historic Acorn Street, Boston

1 Historic Boston

New England's largest city, Boston is nicknamed "the Hub," not just because all New England roads do eventually lead here, but because Bostonians think of their home as the center of all things historical, intellectual, and cultural in the region. Rightly so; Boston's history is inevitably the lead tale in New England's development *(see pp12–13)*.

2 Berkshires

Almost equidistant from Boston to the east and New York City to the south, the Berkshire Hills pledge a wavering allegiance to both. But the Berkshires is a valley kingdom unto itself. Its summer social schedule revolves around the performing arts, but the concentration of resident artists guarantees a rich off-season as well *(see pp32–3)*.

3 Martha's Vineyard
MAP G5

The fish-shaped island of Martha's Vineyard covers 100 sq miles (259 sq km) yet is only 7 miles (11 km) off the mainland. Up Island, the rustic western end, is a serene natural world that includes the sacred striped clay banks of Aquinnah. Down Island, the bustling eastern end, has the town of Vineyard Haven, the old whaling port of Edgartown, and the camp-meeting resort of Oak Bluffs.

Cliffs of Aquinnah, Martha's Vineyard

4 New Bedford
MAP F4

Settled in 1640, this deepwater port at the mouth of Buzzards Bay has always wrested its living from the sea. In the 1840s, pine-masted whaling barks would tie up at the wharves to offload whale oil from a three-year journey *(see p46)*. Today that harbor creaks with great iron fishing boats that dredge the bay for scallops, haul flounder from Nantucket Shoals, or venture offshore for cod and haddock.

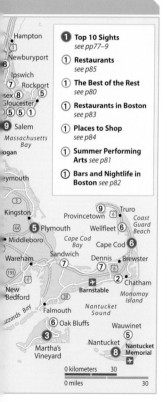

5 Plymouth
MAP G3 ▪ Pilgrim Hall
Museum: 75 Court St, Plymouth;
508 746 1620; open mid-Feb–Dec:
9:30am–4:30pm daily; adm;
www.pilgrimhall.org

Plymouth calls itself "America's
home town," as it was the first
English settlement in New England
and home of the Separatists, who
became known as Pilgrims. The
living history museum of Plimoth
Plantation (see p38) depicts the
settlement around 1627, and
also has exhibits devoted
to Wampanoag life in the
same era. History is
marked with a statue or
plaque on almost every
corner of pleasant modern
Plymouth. Pilgrim Hall
Museum displays artifacts
of the original Pilgrims,
and addresses their story.

6 Cape Cod
English explorer
Bartholomew Gosnold
literally put Cape Cod on
the map in 1602 when he
named the long curl of land for the
fish so abundant in its waters. Cape
Cod's soils are but 15,000 years old –
composed of the sand and gravel
that mark the southernmost advance
of the last glacier – and it is hardly
terra firma; every large storm subtly
reshapes the shore, making peninsulas into islands and vice versa. Yet
the very transience of Cape Cod is
part of its allure (see pp16–17).

Cape Cod, jutting out into the Atlantic

WITCH TRIALS

Salem exhibits mixed feelings about its
witch history. On the 300th anniversary
of the 1692 hysteria that led to the
hanging of 19 "witches" and crushing
of another, the city erected a solemn
memorial to the victims. But come
Halloween, Salem is "witch city,"
capitalizing on its sensational past
to draw curious visitors.

**Artifact at Pilgrim
Hall Museum,
Plymouth**

7 Lowell
MAP F2

Lowell was the first
purpose-built city
in the US, con-
structed in the 1820s
as a large factory town
to manufacture textiles with
equipment designs adapted
from British mills. The textile
industry is gone, but the canal
network and looming mills
remain as testament to the
country's first tryst with the
Industrial Revolution (see
p39). After you've soaked
up the mill history, visit
Jack Kerouac Park (part
of Lowell National Historical Park)
to pay your respects to the Beat
author who was a native son.

8 Nantucket
MAP H5

In contrast with Martha's Vineyard,
only residents bother to bring a car
to tiny Nantucket, as the island lies
30 miles (48 km) offshore and
transportation is expensive. Even
residents tend to bicycle everywhere
(tourists on scooters are scorned).

Explore venerable gray-shingled Nantucket town on foot, starting at the whaling museum (see p46). Then bike to Wauwinet to hike the dunes at Great Point, to Siasconset to see rose-covered cottages, or Surfside to swim or fly kites on the beach.

9 Salem
MAP F2

In the popular imagination, Salem is the city that tried and executed witches. But the 1692 trials are best seen as an aberration in the history of this vibrant city blessed with the art of the Peabody Essex Museum (see p41) and a rich maritime history recounted at the Salem Maritime National Historic Site (see p47). In the early days of the country, Salem's merchant princes were richer than the national treasury. Their grand houses still attest to their power.

Salem Witch Museum

10 Concord and Lexington
MAP E2, F2 ■ Ralph Waldo Emerson House: 28 Cambridge Tpk, Concord; 978 369 2236; open mid-Apr–Oct: 10am–4:30pm Thu–Sat, 1–4:30pm Sun; adm

The opening skirmishes of the American Revolution, in what is now Minute Man National Historical Park (see p38), forever link these neighboring towns. Concord also gave the US its first literary voices in Ralph Waldo Emerson (1803–82) and Henry David Thoreau (1817–62). Also, novelist Louisa May Alcott (1832–88) grew up in Orchard House (see p44). All of the above are buried at Concord's Sleepy Hollow Cemetery.

A DAY PEDALING FROM CAMBRIDGE TO CONCORD

▶ MORNING

Start your 13-mile (21-km) jaunt through American history by taking your bike with you on the T to the Alewife terminus of the Red Line. Follow well-marked signs to the **Minuteman Bikeway**, a flat, paved path. Pedal through Arlington, then watch for egrets, herons, and bobolinks along the edges of **Great Meadows** nature area. The bikeway soon passes the **Lexington Visitors' Center** of **Minute Man National Historical Park** (see p38), perfect for a rest stop. Pick up the park map and brochures, taking note of historic **Lexington Green**, your next stop. Pay homage to the iconic Minute Man statue on the green, then pedal a few blocks up Bedford Street to enjoy deli sandwiches at **Neillio's Gourmet Kitchen** (No. 53).

AFTERNOON

Just west of Lexington Green you switch from the Minuteman Bikeway to **Battle Road Trail**, an unpaved road for walkers and cyclists that parallels the route of the running battle as British forces retreated in 1775; historical signposts explain the significance of sights along the way. **North Bridge**, near another visitor center in the park, is especially evocative. At the end of the trail, follow signs to **The Wayside** and **Orchard House** (see p44) to learn about Concord's 19th-century literary history. Lexington Road takes you into Concord Center, where you and your bike can return to Boston on the commuter rail.

See map on pp76–7

The Best of the Rest

 Gloucester

MAP G2

Sticking 30 miles (42 km) out to sea on Cape Ann, Gloucester's harbor is a legendary fishing port and home to Rocky Neck Art Colony *(see p84)*.

 Northampton and Amherst

MAP C3

The vibrant cultural life of Pioneer Valley revolves around four colleges, including Smith, with its major art museum *(see p42)*. Literary history abounds, as the Emily Dickinson Homestead on Main Street attests.

 Deerfield and the Connecticut Valley

MAP C2 ▪ Historic Deerfield: Old Main Street, Old Deerfield; 413 774 5581; open mid-Apr–late Dec: 9:30am–4:30pm daily; Jan–mid-Apr: call for hours; adm; www.historic-deerfield.org

Settlers braved frequent Indian raids for the rich soil of the Connecticut Valley. Deerfield preserves 60 build-ings from the 17th and 18th centuries.

Springfield

MAP C3 ▪ 800 625 7738 ▪ www.springfieldmuseums.org

Once your kids have climbed on the Dr. Seuss statues at the Quadrangle off State Street, take them to visit the nearby history, art, and natural science museums.

 Rockport

MAP G2

The iconic Motif #1, a red fishing shed in the harbor, is among the most-painted subjects in this lovely village of art galleries and boutiques.

 Mohawk Trail

MAP C2 ▪ www.mohawk trail.com

Drive Route 2 west from Greenfield over the Berkshire Mountains to North Adams to be wowed by some of the area's best fall foliage. Turnoffs lead to orchards and sugar houses.

 Ipswich and Essex

MAP F2, G2

The sands of Crane Beach *(see p52)* in Ipswich and the winding tidal river at Essex *(see p84)* make these North Shore communities great for nature lovers. Both are known for shellfish.

Newburyport

MAP N6

Its fantastic concentration of grand Federal-style homes makes Newburyport an essential stop for history buffs and preservationists. Birders flock to Plum Island at the harbor mouth for some of New England's best birding.

Worcester

MAP E3 ▪ EcoTarium: 222 Harrington Way, Worcester; 508 929 2700; open 10am–5pm Tue–Sat, noon–5pm Sun; adm; www.ecotarium.org

Worcester has a top art museum *(see p40)* and a unique indoor-outdoor museum, the EcoTarium.

Brimfield and Sturbridge

MAP D3

New England's rural heart bustles thrice a year with Brimfield antiques shows *(see p68)*. Old Sturbridge Village *(see p38)* re-creates rural New England of 150 years ago.

Motif #1 in Rockport's harbor

Summer Performing Arts

 Tanglewood
MAP B3 ▪ 297 West St, Lenox
▪ 413 637 1600 ▪ late Jun–early Sep
▪ Adm ▪ www.bso.org
Supreme musicianship and elaborate picnics are equally characteristic of the Boston Symphony's summer home.

Williamstown Theatre Festival

2 **Williamstown Theatre Festival**
MAP B2 ▪ 1000 Main St, Williamstown
▪ 413 597 3400 ▪ Jun–Aug ▪ Adm
▪ www.wtfestival.org
Film and TV directors and actors come here to hone their stagecraft; celebrity-spotting is a summer sport in town when the festival takes place.

3 **Shakespeare & Company**
MAP B3 ▪ 70 Kemble St, Lenox ▪ 413 637 3353 ▪ late May–mid Sep ▪ Adm
▪ www.shakespeare.org
Famed for their Shakespeare performances, this company also develops and produces new plays of social and political significance.

4 **Barrington Stage Company**
MAP B2 ▪ 30 Union St, Pittsfield ▪ 413 236 8888 ▪ mid-Jun–Oct ▪ Adm
▪ www.barringtonstageco.org
A wellspring of new plays and musicals, Barrington Stage incubates electrifying theater that often winds up playing on Broadway.

5 **Gloucester Stage Company**
MAP G2 ▪ 267 E Main St, Gloucester
▪ 978 281 4433 ▪ May–Oct ▪ Adm
▪ www.gloucesterstage.com
Home is a former fish-packing plant adjacent to Rocky Neck Art Colony. Award-winning playwright Israel Horowitz is a company co-founder.

6 **Wellfleet Harbor Actors Theater**
MAP H4 ▪ Rte 6, Wellfleet
▪ 508 349 9428 ▪ May–Oct ▪ Adm
▪ www.what.org
Humor, passion, a sense of the absurd, and a sharp political edge are hallmarks of this small troupe.

7 **Cape Playhouse**
MAP H4 ▪ 820 Rte 6A, Dennis ▪ 508 385 3911 ▪ mid-Jun–Oct, 2nd half Dec ▪ Adm
▪ www.capeplayhouse.com
America's oldest professional summer theater puts on classics, comedies, mysteries, and musicals.

8 **Berkshire Theatre Festival**
MAP B3 ▪ Main St, Stockbridge ▪ 413 997 4444 ▪ mid-Jun–mid-Sep ▪ Adm
▪ www.berkshiretheatregroup.org
The 1888 Stockbridge Casino by noted architect Stanford White makes a grand setting for new, classic, and contemporary theater.

9 **Jacob's Pillow Dance Festival**
MAP B3 ▪ 358 George Carter Rd, Becket ▪ 413 243 9919 ▪ mid-Jun–late Aug ▪ Adm ▪ www.jacobspillow.org
Enjoy performances by leading US and international dance companies in a magical setting.

10 **Blue Hills Bank Pavilion**
MAP F2 ▪ 290 Northern Ave, Boston ▪ 617 728 1600 ▪ Jun–early Sep ▪ Adm ▪ www.livenation.com
This harborside pavilion is a dynamic venue for various performers.

See map on pp76–7

Bars and Nightlife in Boston

The Sinclair
MAP F2 ■ 52 Church St, Cambridge

Part gastropub and part music venue, The Sinclair serves bistro comfort fare as indie bands, Americana musicians, and hipster songwriters entertain.

② Regattabar
MAP F2 ■ Charles Hotel, 1 Bennett St, Cambridge

This intimate room that boasts excellent acoustics is widely acclaimed for presenting some of the best jazz in the country.

③ Beehive
MAP V5 ■ 541 Tremont St

This Bohemian bar-café programs live jazz by local artists. The creative bistro menu is complemented by craft beers and exotic cocktails.

The popular Hawthorne Bar

④ Hawthorne Bar
MAP S5 ■ Hotel Commonwealth, 500a Commonwealth Ave

Some of the country's leading mixologists craft the cocktails in this classy Kenmore Square hotel bar designed for intelligent discussion and wistful flirtation.

⑤ Nick's Comedy Stop
MAP V4 ■ 100 Warrenton St

Nationally known comics from HBO, Showtime, Comedy Central, MTV, and the like headline at this popular spot, which is Boston's longest-running comedy club (since 1977).

Drink, a cocktail landmark

⑥ Drink
MAP X4 ■ 348 Congress St

Fresh herbs, hand-chipped ice, and specialty liqueurs place this hip bar in the vanguard of the cocktail world. Bartenders ask you your mood and then improvise a drink.

⑦ Middle East
MAP S3 ■ 472–480 Massachusetts Ave, Cambridge

If you follow underground music, you're probably already aware of this legendary venue for new bands that are looking to break through.

⑧ Kinsale Irish Pub & Restaurant
MAP W3 ■ 2 Center Plaza, Cambridge St

Built in Ireland, then shipped to Boston and re-assembled, the Kinsale is an authentic piece of the old sod. Live music on Tuesday and Saturday.

⑨ Game On
MAP S5 ■ 82 Lansdowne St

One of sports-crazy Boston's top game-watching spots is built into the walls of Fenway Park. With an entire wall covered with flat-screen TVs, there's always, well, a game on.

⑩ House of Blues®
MAP S5 ■ 15 Lansdowne St

The famed chain sticks to its Boston roots with this cavernous venue.

See map on pp76–7

Restaurants in Boston

1 Menton
MAP X4 ■ 354 Congress St ■ 617 737 0099 ■ Closed L daily ■ $$$

South Boston-raised Barbara Lynch artfully reinvents fine dining at the cusp of French and Italian.

2 Oya
MAP W4 ■ 9 East St ■ 617 654 9900 ■ Closed L daily & Sun–Mon ■ $$$

This contemporary Japanese restaurant is celebrated for chef Tim Cushman's inventive sushi and bounteous *omakase*.

3 Tremont 647
MAP U6 ■ 647 Tremont St ■ 617 226 4600 ■ Closed L Mon–Fri ■ $$

This small, rocking restaurant offers a lively bar scene and adventurous food. Neighborhood foodies adore the weekend pajama brunches.

4 Craigie On Main
MAP S3 ■ 853 Main St ■ 617 497 5511 ■ $$$

Home of the wildly popular gourmet burger. Local chef Tony Maws follows a no-exceptions policy on local, seasonal, and organic ingredients.

5 L'Espalier
MAP U5 ■ 774 Boylston St ■ 617 351 2037 ■ $$$

Come to L'Espalier for impeccable prix-fixe French *haute cuisine* with a New England twist.

6 B+G Oysters
MAP V5 ■ 550 Tremont St ■ 617 423 0550 ■ $$

At least a dozen varieties of oyster are available here, and the sparkling and mineral-rich white wines recommended are a perfect match.

7 Townsman
MAP W4 ■ 120 Kingston St ■ 617 993 0750 ■ Closed L Sat–Sun ■ $$

Located on the Rose Kennedy Greenway, Townsman features nose-to-tail locavore cooking in a brasserie setting with late-night bar.

8 Oleana
MAP S2 ■ 134 Hampshire St, Cambridge ■ 617 661 0505 ■ Closed L ■ $$$

Expect Arab-inspired eastern Mediterranean cuisines at Oleana, featuring spicy dishes from Turkey, Greece, and North Africa. Many diners choose to sit at the outdoor tables in the garden.

9 Mare
MAP X3 ■ 3 Mechanic St ■ 617 723 6273 ■ Closed L ■ $$

Local oysters and crudo plates complement Italian seafood dishes in this chic North End restaurant.

10 Banyan Bar + Refuge
MAP V5 ■ 553 Tremont St ■ 617 556 5611 ■ Closed L, open Sun brunch ■ $$

This modern Asian gastropub hits all the marks with Phillip Tang's skillful blend of East and West.

Asian-inspired Banyan Bar

Places to Shop

1 Faneuil Hall Marketplace

MAP X3 ■ Boston

North and South Markets boast dozens of boutiques and specialty shops. Quincy Market has the city's best food court, as well as more than 40 pushcart vendors selling largely local wares.

2 deCordova I Store

MAP F2 ■ 51 Sandy Pond Rd, Lincoln

Contemporary art, mostly by New England artists, is the focus of deCordova Sculpture Park and Museum. The store at the museum matches that spirit with a range of art supplies, jewelry, wearable art, and inventive educational toys.

3 Fuller Craft Museum
MAP F3 ■ 455 Oak St, Brockton

This premier museum of fine art in craft media carries an extensive selection of artists' jewelry, which is displayed alongside work in glass, ceramic, fiber, and wood.

4 Wrentham Village Premium Outlets
MAP F3 ■ 1 Premium Outlets Blvd, Wrentham

Bargain hunters from all over New England converge on this mall just off I-495, where 170 stores are dedicated to designer apparel and upscale housewares.

5 Rocky Neck Art Colony
MAP G2

It is not difficult to see why this rocky peninsula is such an inspiration to artists. You can walk from cottage to cottage to see (and buy) paintings created by resident painters that belong to one of the oldest operating art colonies in America.

6 Yankee Candle Village
MAP C2 ■ Rtes 5 & 10, South Deerfield

The leading US producer of scented candles offers the world's largest candle selection, home furnishings, food, entertainment, all-year Christmas shopping, and a candle-making museum.

7 Sandwich Glass Museum

MAP G4 ■ 129 Main St, Sandwich

The museum shop carries faithful reproductions of historic pressed glass from Sandwich, an extensive line of American art glass, and blown glass from the museum's own on-site glassblowing studio.

Sandwich Glass Museum

8 Essex
MAP G2

More than 30 antiques shops do business in this historic North Shore community. Keep an eye out to find nautical artifacts, Chinese export porcelain, 18th- and 19th-century furniture, and excellent oil paintings.

9 Provincetown
MAP H3

In summer, Friday is "gallery night" in Provincetown. Galleries along Commercial Street set out wine and cheese to lure prospective buyers.

10 Paradise City Arts Festivals

MAP C3 ■ Rte 9 and Old Ferry Rd, Northampton

Two of the largest gatherings of crafts artists and designers in New England take place over Memorial Day (late May) and Columbus Day (mid-October) weekends at the Three-County Fairgrounds in Northampton, an excellent opportunity to explore and buy local crafts.

Restaurants

PRICE CATEGORIES
For a three course meal for one with half
a bottle of wine (or equivalent meal),
taxes and extra charges.
....
$ under $40 $$ $40–$65 $$$ over $65

1 Mezze Bistro + Bar
MAP B2 ▪ 777 Cold Spring
Rd, Williamstown ▪ 413 458 0123
▪ Closed L ▪ $$
Local growers provide the meat,
produce, and cheeses for this highly
adept American bistro.

2 Cape Sea Grille
MAP H4 ▪ 31 Sea St, Harwich
Port ▪ 508 432 4745 ▪ Closed Jan–mid-
Apr, L & some days spring and fall ▪ $$
Great local fish meets Cape Cod
veggies to spectacular effect for
elegant, candlelit dining.

3 Left Bank, Stonehedge Inn
MAP E2 ▪ 160 Pawtucket Blvd,
Tyngsboro ▪ 978 649 4400 ▪ Open
for B, L, D daily, brunch Sun ▪ $$$
Enjoy lively seasonal cuisine that is
sourced locally, and the best wine
cellar in New England.

Castle Street Café

4 Castle Street Café
MAP B3 ▪ 10 Castle St, Great
Barrington ▪ 413 528 5244 ▪ Closed L,
Sun Nov–Jan ▪ $$
Really taste the Berkshires at this
local favorite which offers a superb
bar menu of classic bistro dishes.

5 Topper's
MAP H5 ▪ 120 Wauwinet Rd,
Nantucket ▪ 508 228 0145 ▪ Closed
late Oct–Apr ▪ $$$
In an idyllic waterfront setting, dine
on Beef Wellington, skillet-roasted
halibut, or buttered lobster with
tortellini in a truffle emulsion.

6 Sweet Life Café
MAP G5 ▪ 63 Circuit Ave, Oak
Bluffs, Martha's Vineyard ▪ 508 696
0200 ▪ Closed L, Mon–Wed May &
Sep–Oct, Nov–Apr ▪ $$$
Local vegetables and fish feature
on the seasonal menu with French,
Italian, and Spanish accents matched
by an extensive wine list.

7 Duckworth's Bistrot
MAP G2 ▪ 197 E Main St,
Gloucester ▪ 978 282 4426 ▪ Closed
L, Mon, Sun Sep–May, Jan ▪ $$
The French-trained chef-owner
offers sumptuous bistro fare –
grilled strip steak, duck breast
with apples, and seafood stew.

8 Il Capriccio
MAP F2 ▪ 888 Main St, Waltham
▪ 781 894 2234 ▪ Closed L, Sun ▪ $$
The elegant Northern Italian menu
changes often, depending on the
New England harvest and the fisher-
men's catch. Extensive wine list.

9 Back Eddy
MAP F4 ▪ 1 Bridge Rd,
Westport ▪ 508 636 6500 ▪ Closed
Mon–Fri L, Jan–Mar ▪ $$
Cutting-edge casual cuisine with a
raw bar of Westport shellfish and
succulent wood-grilled local meats
and fish. The outdoor bar is a
convivial summer social scene.

10 Blue Ginger
MAP F3 ▪ 585 Washington St,
Wellesley ▪ 781 283 5790 ▪ Closed
Sun L ▪ $$$
Celebrity chef Ming Tsai's kitchen
blends Asian and Western influences
in light, spicy, innovative dishes.

See map on pp76–7

⊞ Rhode Island

Rhode Island is not an island at all, but it claims more than its share of dramatic rocky cliffs, sandy beaches, and languid riverbanks. The state was founded by religious dissenters from Massachusetts who chafed at the orthodoxies of Boston and Salem Puritans. The smallest US state, Rhode Island is divided by the very large, fan-shaped Narragansett Bay. At the head of the bay, the capital city of Providence revels in both its Colonial history and its futuristic outlook – the latter courtesy of its colleges and universities. The South County coastline west of the bay features idyllic barrier beaches with long, golden strands and fertile marshes trapped behind high dunes. The mouth of the bay is crossed by stepping-stone islands (and magnificent bridges) that lead to the first home of the US Navy, now the yachting capital of Newport.

Lighthouse, Point Judith

AREA MAP OF RHODE ISLAND

Modern buildings dominating the skyline of Providence

1 Newport

Nineteenth-century mansions and a snug harbor dotted with racing yachts and speedboats make this city one of the great American summer destinations. The downtown area is a history buff's delight *(see pp18–19).*

2 Providence
MAP E4

Rhode Island School of Design (RISD) *(see pp42, 93),* a top US art school, provides zing to downtown Providence, a city also known as a major dining destination. Benefit Street's "Mile of History" captures in its museums and historic houses 250 years of New England life. Visit the traditionally Italian district of Federal Hill for restaurants, salumerias, and coffee shops.

The historic Slater Mill at Pawtucket

3 Pawtucket
MAP E4

So close to Providence that it's hard to distinguish the two, Pawtucket flourished because it sits at the mouth of the Blackstone River, the storied stream of 19th-century industry that drains central New England. Samuel Slater opened the country's first successful cotton mill *(see p39)* here in 1793, jump-starting the American Industrial Revolution. Today it is best known for the minor-league Pawtucket Red Sox *(see p90),* and its September Dragon Boat Race.

Sakonnet Vineyards, Little Compton

4 Tiverton/Little Compton
MAP F4, F5 ■ Carolyn's
Sakonnet Vineyards: 162 W Main Rd,
Little Compton; 800 919 4637; open
late May–mid-Oct: 11am–6pm daily
(to 8pm Thu–Sat); mid-Oct–late May:
11am–5pm daily (to 6pm Fri–Sat);
www.sakonnetwine.com

Occupying their own little peninsula
between Narragansett Bay and the
Massachusetts border, Tiverton *(see
p48)* and Little Compton are insulated
from the modern world by woods and
rolling farmland. Watch for roadside
stands selling seasonal strawberries
and sweet corn. Wine grapes also
flourish. Visit Carolyn's Sakonnet
Vineyards for tours and tastings.

5 Watch Hill
MAP E5

The glorious beaches of South
County, the Rhode Island shore west
of Point Judith, reach their apogee at
Watch Hill, an old-fashioned seaside
community of the town of Westerly.
The village also boasts the charming
Flying Horse Carousel *(see p63)*.

6 Bristol
MAP F4 ■ Herreshoff Marine
Museum: 1 Burnside St; 401 253
5000; open Apr–mid-Dec: 10am–5pm
daily; adm; www.herreshoff.org
■ Blithewold Mansion & Gardens: 101
Ferry Rd; 401 253 2707; open Apr–
May: 11am–5pm Tue–Sun; Jun–mid-
Oct: 10am–4pm Tue–Sat (to 3pm
Sun); adm; www.blithewold.org

Renowned for jubilant Independence
Day celebrations that date from
1785 *(see p72)*, Bristol is a charming

deep-water seaport on the east
side of Narragansett Bay. The village
is home to the Herreshoff yacht-
building firm, whose museum also
traces the history of the America's
Cup, the most prestigious prize in
yacht-racing. Visit the house and
gardens of the Blithewold estate,
where Rhode Island brides flock
to wed with spectacular vistas of
Narragansett Bay as a backdrop.

7 Block Island
MAP E6 ■ Block Island
Ferry: Pt Judith; 401 783 7996;
www.blockislandferry.com

Just 15 miles (24 km) off the coast,
Block Island has long been a summer
vacation haven for New Englanders. A
quarter of its land is protected against
development (zoning prohibits modern
structures), and 30 miles (48 km) of
nature trails crisscross the pear-
shaped island. Crescent Beach, just
north of the Victorian resort village of
Old Harbor, has fabulous swimming
and – when the surf is right – good
surfing. Deep-sea fishing excursions
are popular day-trips from Old Harbor.

8 Narragansett/Point Judith
MAP E5

In 1900, a fire destroyed the hotels
and casino that made Narragansett
Beach a high-society resort. Today,
families and sunbathers rule the

WHAT A SPAN!

Constructed 1966–9, Newport's
Claiborne Pell Bridge is the longest
bridge in Rhode Island and the largest
suspension bridge in New England. With
a main span of 1,601 ft (488 m) and an
overall length of 11,247 ft (3,428 m), the
bridge arcs over Narragansett Bay to
connect Jamestown and Newport.

beach while surfers in wetsuits ride the waves. The peninsula going south ends at Point Judith, which shelters the fishing port of Galilee. Whale-watching and deep-sea-fishing cruise vessels share berths with the fishing boats. Don't miss fish dinner at George's of Galilee *(see pp67 & 92)*.

⑨ Wickford
MAP E5 ■ Kayak Centre of Rhode Island: 9 Phillips St; 401 295 4400; daily year-round; adm; www.kayakcentre.com

Artists and craftspeople have flocked to this historic, picturesque village near North Kingstown, and their galleries and shops are big lures for daytrippers. What few visitors realize is that Wickford's location on the west side of Narragansett Bay makes it the ideal launching point for exploring the bay by sea kayak. Inquire about expert guided paddles at the Kayak Centre.

Frosty Drew Observatory, Charlestown

⑩ Charlestown
MAP E5 ■ Frosty Drew Observatory: 61 Park Ln, Ninigret Park; 401 364 9508; open clear Fri nights; www.frostydrew.org

It can be hard to tell whether Charlestown is land or water, as the 4-mile (6.5-km) coastline encompasses the largest saltwater marshes in the state. You'll find some of New England's best birding for wading birds and waterfowl in this watery ecosystem between land and sea. Sprawling Ninigret Park has tracks for cyclists and bladers as well as a swimming pool and tennis courts. Every clear Friday night, join the astronomy buffs at Frosty Drew Observatory to scan the skies.

NAVIGATING FROM PROVIDENCE TO NEWPORT

▶ MORNING

Start the day in **Providence** *(see p87)* with a stroll around **Waterplace Park**, a broad pool and amphitheater between Francis and Exchange streets. Cross the Steeple Street Bridge, noting the soaring Ionic columns of the **First Baptist Church in America** on your left. Pop into **Café Choklad** (12 Thomas St) for brioche and hot chocolate before entering the **RISD Museum** *(see p42)*, paying special attention to the contemporary art in many different media. The attached store specializes in creations by RISD-affiliated designers.

AFTERNOON

Take I-195 east to Rte 136 south to reach picturesque **Bristol** *(see p88)*. Eat stuffies (stuffed clams) for lunch at **Thames Waterside Bar & Grill** (251 Thames St) and see the America's Cup exhibits at the **Herreshoff Marine Museum** (1 Burnside St) before continuing south on Rte 114 to **Newport** *(see pp18–19)*. Take a Gilded Age mansion tour of **The Breakers** (44 Ochre Pt Ave) and get seats on a sunset cruise in Newport harbor (Bannisters Wharf) aboard a schooner or a motor yacht.

EVENING

Make a night of it at **The Landing** (30 Bowen's Wharf), a large and entertaining waterfront eating and drinking establishment known for its raw bar, live music, and maritime-themed cocktails.

See map on pp86–7

The Best of the Rest

1 Audubon Society of Rhode Island Environmental Education Center

MAP F4 ▪ 1401 Hope St, Rte 114, Bristol ▪ 401 245 7500 ▪ Open mid-Apr–mid-Oct: daily; mid-Oct–mid-Apr: Wed–Sun ▪ Adm ▪ www.asri.org

Explore marine life at this family-friendly wildlife refuge.

Green Animals Topiary Garden

2 Green Animals Topiary Garden

MAP F5 ▪ 380 Cory's Lane, off Rte 114, Portsmouth ▪ 401 847 1000 ▪ Open late May–early Oct: daily ▪ Adm ▪ www.newportmansions.org

A Rhode Island Red rooster is one of the 80 topiaries at the US's oldest topiary garden, located on a small country estate in Portsmouth.

3 Beavertail Lighthouse Museum

MAP E5 ▪ Beavertail State Park, Jamestown ▪ 401 423 3270 ▪ Open Jun–Sep: daily; Oct: Sat & Sun ▪ Adm ▪ www.beavertaillight.org

There has been a lighthouse on this site since 1749. The keeper's house is now a museum.

4 Casey Farm

MAP E5 ▪ 2325 Boston Neck Rd, Saunderstown (North Kingstown) ▪ 401 295 1030 ▪ Open Jun–mid-Oct: Mon–Fri ▪ Adm

This 18th-century farmhouse offers a glimpse into Rhode Island's agricultural past. Produce grown here is sold on Saturdays.

5 City Center Ice Rink

MAP E4 ▪ 2 Kennedy Plaza, Providence ▪ 401 331 5544 ▪ Open late Nov–early Mar: daily ▪ Adm ▪ provparks conservancy.org/visit/ice-skating

Skate in the shadow of the state's tallest skyscraper, the 428-ft (130-m) Art Deco "Superman Building."

6 Pawtuxet Village

MAP E4 ▪ Warwick

A mid-June parade marks the 1772 burning of a British ship by local patriots. Dozens of Colonial buildings feature in the historic district.

7 Museum of Work and Culture

MAP E3 ▪ 42 S Main St, Woonsocket ▪ 401 769 9675 ▪ Closed Mon ▪ Adm ▪ www.rihs.org

This museum in a former textile mill details the lives of those who worked here and in other local factories.

8 Gilbert Stuart Birthplace and Museum

MAP E5 ▪ 815 Gilbert Stuart Rd, Saunderstown ▪ 401 294 3001 ▪ Open May–mid-Jun, Sep–mid-Oct: Thu–Mon; mid-Jun–Aug: daily ▪ Adm ▪ www.gilbertstuartmuseum.org

Artist Gilbert Stuart (1755–1828) painted the celebrities of his day. A tour of his birthplace uncovers his modest beginnings.

9 East Bay Bike Path

MAP F4

Zip down the bayside path between East Providence and Bristol for views of Narragansett Bay on one side, herons and egrets on the other.

10 Pawtucket Red Sox Baseball, McCoy Stadium

MAP E4 ▪ 1 Columbus Ave, Pawtucket ▪ 401 724 7300 ▪ Open Apr–Sep ▪ Adm ▪ www.pawsox.com

Many top baseball players perfected their game with this Boston Triple-A team. Grab a seat in McCoy Stadium and you might spot the next star.

See map on pp86–7

Restaurants

PRICE CATEGORIES

For a three course meal for one with half
a bottle of wine (or equivalent meal),
taxes and extra charges.

$ under $40 $$ $40–$65 $$$ over $65

1 White Horse Tavern
MAP F5 ■ 26 Marlborough St,
Newport ■ 401 849 3600 ■ Closed
Sun L; open Sun brunch ■ $$$

America's oldest tavern, with beamed
ceilings, log fires, and candlelit tables,
offers classic American cuisine.

2 Le Central
MAP F4 ■ 483 Hope St, Bristol
■ 401 396 9965 ■ Closed Sun–Mon
■ $$

East Bay (as in Narragansett) meets
Left Bank (as in Paris) at this French
bistro with a short menu of excellent
comfort food (such as cassoulet with
duck confit) and great local fish.

3 Trio
MAP E5 ■ 15 Kingstown Rd,
Narragansett ■ 401 792 4333 ■ $$

Eat chops, pasta, and seafood at
bargain prices or dig into a juicy rib-
eye steak or pan-seared scallops.

4 Al Forno
MAP E4 ■ 577 S Main St,
Providence ■ 401 273 9760 ■ Closed
Tue–Sat L, Sun, Mon ■ $$

Al Forno has a great reputation for
its tasty baked pastas and meats
roasted in a wood-fired oven.

5 Seasons at Ocean House
MAP E5 ■ 1 Bluff Ave, Westerly
■ 401 584 7000 ■ Closed Sun L, D
Mon–Tue ■ $$$

This hotel restaurant
has an open kitchen

that lets diners watch the chefs
prepare elegant seasonal American
dishes with creative touches.

6 New Rivers
MAP E4 ■ 7 Steeple St, Providence
■ 401 751 0350 ■ Closed L, Sun D ■ $$

Spicy contemporary cooking at its
best pairs with an intimate dining
space for a truly romantic experience.

7 Chez Pascal
MAP E4 ■ 960 Hope St,
Providence ■ 401 421 4422 ■ Closed
L, Sun ■ $$

The chef-owner of this unabashedly
Burgundian bistro makes his own
pâtés, sausages, and confits. Share
a charcuterie appetizer then follow
it up with the pork of the day.

8 Wright's Farm Restaurant
MAP E4 ■ 84 Inman Rd, Harrisville
■ 401 769 2856 ■ Closed Mon–Fri L,
Mon–Wed D ■ $

This 1,000-seater is the best of the
Rhode Island "all-you-can-eat
chicken dinner" restaurants.

9 Restaurant 1879, Atlantic Inn
MAP E6 ■ High St, Block Island
■ 401 466 5883 ■ Closed L all year;
late Apr–late May & Sep–late Oct
Mon–Wed D ■ $$

Fish and farm produce feature on the
menu at this contemporary American
eatery. The verandah tables offer
spectacular views of the sunset.

10 Simone's
MAP F4 ■ 275 Child St, Warren
■ 401 247 1200 ■ Closed L, Mon;
open brunch Fri–Sun ■ $$

Dinner features inventive American
fare with Mediterranean accents,
but chef Joe Simone's first love is
spicy brunch plates.

**Ocean House,
perched on a bluff**

Cafés and Bars

 Perks & Corks
MAP E5 ▪ 48 High St, Westerly
By day, Perks & Corks is a slacker's dream of a coffee bar, with smooth lattes, free Wi-Fi, and enveloping sofas. Then after dark it morphs into a bar serving wines by the glass and killer cocktails.

2 Chan's Fine Oriental Dining
MAP E3 ▪ 267 Main St, Woonsocket
Known for its "eggroll jazz," Chan's really hops on the weekends when blues bands and small jazz combos set the diners' fingers snapping. The Chinese fare draws on several regional cuisines.

3 Fluke Wine, Bar & Kitchen
MAP F5 ▪ 41 Bowen's Wharf, Newport
Catch the sunset sitting at this atmospheric bar on Newport Harbor, while enjoying a glass of chardonnay with a bowl of steamed clams.

4 22 Bowen's Wine Bar and Grille
MAP F5 ▪ 22 Bowen's Wharf, Newport
More than 600 wines make this bar and steakhouse a wine-lover's oasis. Watch boat traffic in the harbor, while tucking into prime rib or slurping down oysters.

Outside dining at 22 Bowen's

5 Trinity Brewhouse
MAP E4 ▪ 186 Fountain St, Providence
Trinity is a "United Nations" of beer; its ales, lagers, and stout made on the premises recall English, German, and Irish styles. It's a popular after-show venue with playgoers at Trinity Repertory Theatre.

6 Olympia Tea Room
MAP E5 ▪ 74 Bay St, Watch Hill
Score one of the outdoor tables at this delightful spot near the Flying Horses Carousel, and you can watch the action while you sip white wine and eat roasted clams with linguine.

7 Scales & Shells
MAP F5 ▪ 527 Thames St, Newport
After the dinner rush, this all-fish restaurant turns into a convivial bar where patrons can enjoy local shellfish from the raw bar with a glass of wine or beer.

8 George's of Galilee
MAP E5 ▪ 250 Sand Hill Cove Rd, Galilee
Stop off here to savor the pick of the catch from the Galilee fishermen; many spend their evenings at the bar.

9 Costantino's Venda Ravioli
MAP E4 ▪ 265 Atwells Ave, Providence
This Italian gourmet shop, with a huge selection of pastas, cheeses, and sausages, also serves coffee and food at tables in the back.

10 McKinley's Waterfront
MAP E4 ▪ 1 Division St, East Greenwich
This warm Irish pub is a welcome find on a cool winter night, especially thanks to more than 20 ales on tap. In summer, the outdoor seating overlooking Greenwich Bay is an ideal spot to sip a brew and watch the sailboats go by.

Places to Shop

Colorful display at RISD Works

1 RISD Works
MAP E4 ■ Chace Center, 20 N Main St, Providence ■ Closed Mon

Creativity abounds at the RISD Works, the RISD Museum *(see p42)* store, which showcases fashion, furniture, toys, and tools from alumni and faculty members of the school.

2 The Fantastic Umbrella Factory
MAP E5 ■ 4820 Old Post Rd, Charlestown

No umbrellas are made here and it isn't a factory. It's actually a maze of unusual little shops selling work by local craftsmen and artists, novelty gifts, ethnic treasures, and even pots and plants.

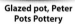

Glazed pot, Peter Pots Pottery

3 Brown & Hopkins Country Store
MAP E4 ■ 1179 Putnam Pike, Chepachet

Children can select from the "penny candy" counter while their parents browse the home furnishings and accessories at this historic store.

4 Bowen's Wharf
MAP F5 ■ America's Cup Ave, Newport

Shops on this 18th-century wharf have a nautical flavor. Landlubbers can easily outfit themselves to look like seasoned sailors.

5 Warren
MAP F4

If it's old, you'll probably find it here. A cluster of shops in the compact downtown area of this former whaling port and mill town have turned it into a collector's paradise.

6 Gray's Grist Mill
MAP F5 ■ Adamsville Rd, Adamsville

For cornmeal to make jonnycakes *(see p65)* at home, stop at this old mill on a weekend to see local flint corn ground between immense stones from France.

7 Peter Pots Pottery
MAP E5 ■ 494 Glen Rock Rd, West Kingston

Collectors favor the modern lines and distinctive glazes of Peter Pots Pottery, founded in 1948. The studio, in an 18th-century mill building, displays the complete line of dinnerware and decorative pieces.

8 Pier Marketplace
MAP E5 ■ Narragansett Town Beach, Narragansett

On breaks from the beach, sunbathers browse the resort wear and gift shops here, then treat themselves to ice cream or a bag of saltwater taffy.

9 Providence Place
MAP E4 ■ 1 Providence Place, Providence

This shopping mall in the heart of downtown Providence overlooks Waterfront Park, and has every local and national chain you could ask for.

10 Garden City Center
MAP E4 ■ Rte 2, Cranston

This outdoors village-like complex 7 miles (11 km) from Providence offers the same range of shops and dining that you'll find in enclosed malls.

See map on pp86–7

TOP10 **Connecticut**

The Connecticut River touches four states, but only gives its name to one. Settlers from Boston established Hartford on the riverbank in 1635, ultimately creating the first fully articulated constitution in the American colonies. Three years later, more Bostonians pitched their tents on Long Island Sound and created New Haven, where a small school moved in 1716 and blossomed into Yale University. Harnessing the river for power, Connecticut inventors proved some of the country's most ingenious entrepreneurs. But Connecticut is as beautiful as it is industrious, as American artists demonstrated a century ago when they painted the upland woods and the green and gold marshes of Long Island Sound.

**State Capitol,
Hartford**

AREA MAP OF CONNECTICUT

① Top 10 Sights *see pp95-7*		① Places to Shop *see p103*	
① Fine Dining *see p100*		① Gardens and House Museums *see p98*	
① Children's Activities *see p99*		① Casual Dining *see p101*	
① Cafés and Bars *see p102*			

Roses in Elizabeth Park, Hartford

 Hartford
MAP C4

As the state capital, Hartford has many grand buildings and institutions, from the Victorian-Gothic Connecticut State Capitol in Bushnell Park to the public art museum, Wadsworth Atheneum *(see p41)*, founded in 1842. Hartford was also a hotbed of 19th-century publishing and writing. The Mark Twain House *(see p45)*, where America's greatest yarn-spinner and frontier humorist enjoyed a later life of middle-class comfort, and the Gothic-Revival-style Harriet Beecher Stowe Center *(see p98)* next door underscore the city's literary prominence. Smell the roses – more than 800 varieties of them – in Elizabeth Park, whose rose garden was created in 1904 *(see p98)*.

New Haven
MAP C5 ■ Yale Peabody Museum of Natural History: 170 Whitney Ave; 203 432 5050; open 10am–5pm Tue–Sat, noon–5pm Sun; adm; www.yale.edu/peabody

Since the Collegiate School moved to town in 1716, town and gown have been inextricably linked in New Haven. Collections at the Yale University Art Museums *(see p42)* and the Yale Peabody Museum of Natural History put larger cities to shame. The town's culinary legacy includes the legendary pizzas of Frank Pepe *(see p101)*.

Yale University Art Gallery, New Haven

Wethersfield
MAP C4

The epitome of Colonial and Federal style, the center of Old Wethersfield has a genteel grace that belies its early history as a frontier community beleaguered by Indian attacks. The distinctive architecture lining the community's broad streets and the weathered headstones of its cemetery make Old Wethersfield a great destination for Colonial history buffs.

Roseland Cottage, Quiet Corner

4 Quiet Corner
MAP D4

The unassuming nickname for Connecticut's northeastern corner suggests that little of excitement has happened here since General Israel Putnam killed the last wolf in the state and made it safe for sheep-farming. In truth, this area of bucolic repose is dotted with the homes of former country squires, including the flamboyant Roseland Cottage Bowen House (see p98). The region is often overlooked, but antiques hunters always stop in Putnam (see p103).

5 New London and Groton
MAP D5

The deepwater port at the mouth of the Thames River – Groton on the east side, New London on the west – lies roughly halfway between Boston and New York. It was a key base of operations for the American Navy during the Revolution; nowadays, ocean cruise ships call here. The massive shipyards of Electric Boat, builder of nuclear-powered submarines, lie in Groton. Explore the Submarine Force Museum (see p47), home of the world's first nuclear-powered sub, the USS *Nautilus*.

6 Lower Connecticut River
MAP D5 ■ Connecticut River Museum: 67 Main St, Essex; 860 767 8269; open 10am–5pm Tue–Sun (late May–early Sep daily); adm; www.ctrivermuseum.org

Designated as a "last great place" by the Nature Conservancy, the lower reaches of the Connecticut River, from East Haddam to Lyme, have a magical beauty that captivates artists and sustains fish and wildlife, including large numbers of bald eagles in the winter. See how the American Impressionists captured the scene at the Florence Griswold Museum (see p98) in Old Lyme, and explore the rich history and fascinating ecology of the region at the Connecticut River Museum in Essex.

7 Gold Coast
MAP B6

The communities that lie along the New Haven commuter rail line from Greenwich north to Norwalk are the wealthiest in Connecticut – hence the nickname "Gold Coast." When residents want to shop, they head to Greenwich, where boutiques cater to hedge fund millionaires. To dine or to party, they usually make a beeline for South Norwalk, where a bustling bar and restaurant scene has taken hold.

8 Midcoast Beaches
MAP C6

The great shield of Long Island shelters the sandy shoreline between New Haven Harbor and the mouth of the Connecticut River at Old Lyme (see p48). Protected from storms and erosion, the barrier beaches feature soft sand and gentle surf. Many private beach communities are located here, but so are the

AMISTAD AND FREEDOM

In July 1839, African slaves aboard the schooner *Amistad* revolted and were taken into custody at New Haven. Two years of legal battles ensued in New Haven and Hartford, but the slaves won their freedom. Several memorials stand in Connecticut, and a replica ship makes New Haven its home port.

The port of Mystic

main state-owned beaches, which include the 2-mile (3-km) strand at Hammonasset Beach State Park *(see p53)*. Communities like Branford and Clinton live for the sweet but brief summer. Shops are often seasonal.

9 **Litchfield Hills**

Stretching west from the Connecticut River to the New York border, the Litchfield Hills are Connecticut's proper, manicured mountains. Model 18th- and 19th-century communities of white houses and white churches cluster around tidy town greens. In spring, waterfalls roar off the hillsides and you'll find hardy fishermen wading cold mountain brooks to cast flies for trout. In summer, the smell of newly mown lawns and the sweet scents of perennial flower gardens perfume the air *(see pp24–5)*.

Waterfall, Litchfield Hills

10 **Mystic and Stonington**
MAP D5, E5

Small seafaring ports of the eastern Connecticut coast, Stonington and Mystic diverged when the latter developed as a tourism center *(see p46)*. Quieter Stonington, 4 miles (6.5 km) away, retains all the hallmarks of a 19th-century fishing and shipping port, and is dotted with upscale boutiques, cheery cafés, and bars where fishermen and antiques dealers drink side by side.

A DRIVING TOUR FROM TALL SHIPS TO SUBMARINES

Submarine Force Museum
Thames River
12
95
Mystic River
Mystic Seaport
New London
Mystic Pizza
Mystic
1
Custom House Maritime Museum
Stonington

▶ **MORNING**

Begin the day by exploring the picturesque fishing and erstwhile shipping village of **Stonington**. Many a tall ship for whaling and overseas trade was constructed along the Mystic River here. To get more of a feel for those maritime days, drive downriver 4 miles (6.5 km) to the village of **Mystic** (which is half in Groton, half in Stonington). Spend the rest of the morning exploring the vessels and the re-created village of **Mystic Seaport** *(see p46)*. Make sure you tour the *Charles W Morgan*, the last surviving wooden whaling ship.

AFTERNOON

Pick up some slices from **Mystic Pizza** (56 W Main St) and follow Rte 1 west through the coastal plain to the **Submarine Force Museum** *(see p47)*. This is where the American nuclear-powered submarine program unfolded after World War II. Tour the first vessel (the USS *Nautilus*) and try your hand at the simulated controls of a complex modern submarine. Just across the Thames River lies the historic town of **New London** *(see p96)*, where you can continue your maritime-themed tour at the **Custom House Maritime Museum** (150 Bank St), which also offers visitors light-house tours and boat trips.

Pizza at Mystic Pizza

See map on pp94–5 ←

Gardens and House Museums

① **Roseland Cottage Bowen House**

MAP D4 ▪ 556 Rte 169, Woodstock ▪ 860 928 4074 ▪ Open Jun–mid Oct: Wed–Sun ▪ Adm ▪ www.historic newengland.org

This pink, Gothic-style cottage was the summer getaway for the wealthy Bowen family of New York.

Bush-Holley Historic Site

② **Bush-Holley Historic Site**

MAP A6 ▪ 39 Strickland Rd, Cos Cob ▪ 203 869 6899 ▪ Open Wed–Sun (Jan–Feb: Sat–Sun) ▪ Adm by guided tour ▪ www.hstg.org

This interesting museum pinpoints two revolutions in Cos Cob: the political upheaval of the 1770s and the artistic ferment of American Impressionism, 125 years later.

③ **Bartlett Arboretum**

MAP A6 ▪ 151 Brookdale Rd, Stamford ▪ 203 322 6971 ▪ Open daily ▪ www.bartlettarboretum.org

Woodlands, wetlands, meadows, and formal gardens make a living museum of 850 specimen trees.

④ **Florence Griswold Museum**

MAP D5 ▪ 96 Lyme St, Old Lyme ▪ 860 434 5542 ▪ Closed Mon ▪ Adm ▪ www.florencegriswoldmuseum.org

View the history of American Impressionism at this former rooming house, where artist-boarders painted more than 40 panels on the walls.

⑤ **Elizabeth Park Rose Gardens**

MAP C4 ▪ Prospect Ave, Hartford ▪ Open daily ▪ www.elizabethparkct.org

In June, plants burst into bloom here, the US's oldest municipal rose garden.

⑥ **Hill-Stead Museum**

MAP C4 ▪ 35 Mountain Rd, Farmington ▪ 860 677 4787 ▪ Closed Mon ▪ Adm ▪ www.hillstead.org

This hilltop estate is an aristocratic world of privilege and elegance.

⑦ **Glebe House Museum & Gertrude Jekyll Garden**

MAP B5 ▪ 49 Hollow Rd, Woodbury ▪ 203 263 2855 ▪ Open May–Oct: Wed–Sun ▪ Adm ▪ www.glebehouse museum.org

This 1750 home has the only US garden created by famed British designer Gertrude Jekyll.

⑧ **Lockwood-Mathews Mansion Museum**

MAP B6 ▪ 295 West Ave, Norwalk ▪ 203 838 9799 ▪ Open Apr–Jan: Wed–Sun ▪ Adm ▪ www.lockwood mathewsmansion.com

Decorative excesses abound at this estate, built for a wealthy banker and railroad tycoon.

⑨ **Harriet Beecher Stowe Center**

MAP C4 ▪ 77 Forest St, Hartford ▪ 860 522 9258 ▪ Open daily (Jan–Mar: closed Tue) ▪ Adm ▪ www.harrietbeecherstowecenter.org

Stowe, author of *Uncle Tom's Cabin*, moved here, her last home, in 1873.

⑩ **Bellamy-Ferriday House & Garden**

MAP B4 ▪ 9 Main St N, Bethlehem ▪ 203 266 7596 ▪ Open May–Sep: Fri–Mon; Oct: Sat–Sun ▪ Adm ▪ www.ctlandmarks.org

Built for a legendary preacher in the 18th century, the final owner was a civil rights activist.

Children's Activities

1 Connecticut's Beardsley Zoo

MAP B6 ■ 1875 Noble Ave, Bridgeport ■ 203 394 6565 ■ Open daily ■ Adm ■ www.beardsleyzoo.org

Siberian tigers are the top cats at this 300-animal zoo. Also spy on the wolves from the observation area.

2 International Skating Center of Connecticut

MAP C4 ■ 1375 Hopmeadow St, Simsbury ■ 860 651 5400 ■ Call for public skating hours ■ Adm ■ www.isccskate.com

Many Olympic skaters train at this top ice rink that allows public skating.

3 Maritime Aquarium at Norwalk

MAP B6 ■ 10 N Water St, Norwalk ■ 203 852 0700 ■ Open daily ■ Adm ■ www.maritimeaquarium.org

This aquatic center highlights the creatures in its own backyard, like harbor seals and sand tiger sharks.

4 UConn Animal Barns and Dairy Bar

MAP D4 ■ University of Connecticut, Storrs ■ Animal barn: 860 486 2023 ■ Dairy bar: 860 486 2634 ■ Open daily

Watch the cows being milked, then head to the dairy bar for freshly made farm ice cream.

5 Mashantucket Pequot Museum

MAP D5 ■ 110 Pequot Trail, Mashantucket ■ 800 411 9671 ■ Open Wed–Sat ■ Adm ■ www.pequotmuseum.org

This museum recounts the area's history from the perspective of its pre-colonial inhabitants.

6 Ocean Beach Park

MAP D5 ■ 98 Neptune Ave, New London ■ 860 447 3031 ■ Open late May–early Sep ■ Adm ■ www.ocean-beach-park.com

Kids' paradise with a waterslide, beach, miniature golf, and rides.

7 The Dinosaur Place

MAP D5 ■ 1650 Rte 85, Montville ■ 860 443 4367 ■ Park open Apr–Nov, store year-round ■ Adm ■ www.thedinosaurplace.com

Every child loves a dinosaur, and over 40 life-sized concrete dinosaurs wait to be discovered here, along nature trails through lush woodlands.

8 Essex Steam Train and Riverboat

MAP D5 ■ 1 Railroad Ave, Essex ■ 860 767 0103 or 800 377 3987 ■ Open May–Oct, Dec ■ Adm ■ www.essexsteamtrain.com

Take the throttle in a diesel-train simulator, before riding a vintage train and a riverboat along the Connecticut River.

9 New England Air Museum

MAP C4 ■ 36 Perimeter Rd, Bradley International Airport, Windsor Locks ■ 860 623 3305 ■ Open daily ■ Adm ■ www.neam.org

It's hard to tell if dads or kids get more out of the 65 aircraft and 200 or so engines that are on show here.

Aircraft, New England Air Museum

10 Children's Museum

MAP C4 ■ 950 Trout Brook Dr, W Hartford ■ 203 231 2824 ■ Open Tue–Sun (Jul–Aug: daily) ■ Adm ■ www.thechildrensmuseumct.org

Featuring a planetarium, a wildlife sanctuary, and a wide variety of interactive exhibits, this museum delights and educates kids of all ages.

See map on pp94–5

Fine Dining

1 Oyster Club
MAP D5 ▪ 13 Water St, Mystic ▪ 860 415 9266 ▪ Closed Mon–Thu L ▪ $$

Restaurant and raw bar that specializes in fresh seafood. The menu showcases the produce of local farmers and fishermen.

2 Union League Café
MAP C5 ▪ 1032 Chapel St, New Haven ▪ 203 562 4299 ▪ Closed Sat L, Sun ▪ $$$

The French chef-owner of Union League brings the hearty, market-driven cuisine of a Parisian brasserie to the sophisticated streets of New Haven near Yale University.

3 Max Downtown
MAP C4 ▪ City Place, 185 Asylum St, Hartford ▪ 860 522 2530 ▪ Closed Sat & Sun L ▪ $$

Tasty beef ranges from petite steak *au poivre* to giant porterhouse at this bustling urban chophouse.

4 Cottage Restaurant and Café
MAP C4 ▪ 427 Farmington Ave, Plainville ▪ 860 793 8888 ▪ Closed Sat L, Sun, Mon ▪ $$

Years in New Orleans gave the New American cooking of the chef-owner a Cajun accent. Gourmet cuisine at budget prices – and her bartender brother mixes a mean cocktail.

5 85 Main
MAP D4 ▪ 85 Main St, Putnam ▪ 860 928 1660 ▪ $$

Sample the superb seafood in either the cozy dining room or the blue-and-white tiled bar.

6 Hopkins Inn
MAP B4 ▪ 22 Hopkins Rd, New Preston ▪ 860 868 7295 ▪ Open B, L, D Tue–Sun (Jan–late Mar: Tue–Sat) ▪ $$

The menu is laden with Austrian fare such as schnitzel and sweetbreads. The wine selection follows suit.

7 Good News Café
MAP B5 ▪ 694 Main St S, Woodbury ▪ 203 266 4663 ▪ Closed Tue ▪ $$

The chef-owner insists on only local, sustainable, organic products, but her food is never precious, just delicious.

8 Match
MAP B6 ▪ 98 Washington St, S Norwalk ▪ 203 852 1088 ▪ Closed L ▪ $$

Sparkling seafood dishes, inventive seasonal American fare, and rich desserts are a perfect match to the hippest bar on SoNo's restaurant row.

9 Bar Americain
MAP D5 ▪ 1 Mohegan Sun Blvd, Uncasville ▪ 860 862 8000 ▪ Closed L ▪ $$$

Glitzy environs and expertly executed French and American classics from acclaimed celebrity chef, Bobby Flay.

10 Harbour House Restaurant
MAP D5 ▪ Inn at Mystic, 3 Williams Ave, Mystic ▪ 860 536 8140 ▪ Closed L Mon–Fri ▪ $$

Classic seafood, wood-fired pizzas, a great raw bar, and craft beer make this waterfront dining room a local favorite. Juicy steaks also help.

Great views from Harbour House

Casual Dining

PRICE CATEGORIES
For a three course meal for one with half
a bottle of wine (or equivalent meal),
taxes and extra charges.
....
$ under $40 **$$** $40–$65 **$$$** over $65

1 Frank Pepe Pizzeria Napoletana
MAP C5 ■ 157 Wooster St, New Haven
■ 203 865 5762 ■ $
The thin-crust pizza at this no-frills
joint open since 1925 has an almost
cult following among Yale students.
White clam pizza (no tomato sauce)
is among the most popular.

2 O'Rourke's Diner
MAP C5 ■ 728 Main St,
Middletown ■ 860 346 6101 ■ Open
5am–2pm Sun–Thu, 5am–9pm Fri–
Sat ■ $
At this classic diner, dating from the
mid-1940s, some of the best food
comes fresh off the grill.

3 Rawley's Drive-In
MAP B6 ■ 1886 Post Rd, Rte 1,
Fairfield ■ 203 259 9023 ■ Open
11am–6:30pm Mon–Sat ■ $
When customers stand in line for
20 minutes, it's clear a restaurant is
doing something right. It's the hot dogs
that keep them coming back for more.

4 The Cookhouse
MAP B5 ■ 31 Danbury Rd,
New Milford ■ 860 355 4111 ■ $
Wood-smoked barbecued meat is
nearly a religion here. Top sellers are
slow-roasted beef brisket, pork back
ribs, and Carolina-style pulled pork.

5 Captain Scott's Lobster Dock
MAP D5 ■ 80 Hamilton St, New
London ■ 860 439 1741 ■ Open Apr–
mid-Oct: 11am–9pm daily ■ Closed
mid-Oct–Mar ■ $
Known for its hot lobster rolls with
butter and lobster salad, this seafood
shack on a working harbor has an
authenticity few can match.

Pizza lovers at Mystic Pizza

6 Mystic Pizza
MAP D5 ■ 56 W Main St,
Mystic ■ 860 536 3700 ■ $
A Julia Roberts movie made this
pizza-and-pasta joint famous, but
diners keep returning for the "secret
recipe" tomato sauce that's gene-
rously slathered on the pizzas.

7 Shady Glen
MAP C4 ■ 840 E Middle
Turnpike, Manchester ■ 860 649 4245
■ Open B, L, D daily ■ $
The homemade ice cream is great,
but it's the cheeseburgers that are
really the top stars here.

8 Blackie's Hot Dog Stand
MAP C5 ■ 2200 Waterbury Rd,
Cheshire ■ 203 699 1819 ■ Closed Fri
■ $
Since 1928, Blackie's has offered hot
dogs with or without homemade
spicy pepper relish, birch beer on
tap, and chocolate milk.

9 Rein's
MAP C4 ■ 435 Hartford
Turnpike, Vernon ■ 860 875 1344 ■ $
This central Connecticut spot makes
better Jewish deli food, including
latkes, than most of New York, and
is just a quick stop off highway I-84.

10 West Street Grill
MAP B4 ■ 43 West St, Litchfield
■ 860 567 3885 ■ $$
Casual lunches are a big hit here,
especially the burgers and the pulled
short-rib beef sandwich.

See map on pp94–5 ←

Cafés and Bars

Stylish interiors at Max's Oyster Bar

1 Max's Oyster Bar
MAP C4 ■ 964 Farmington Ave,
West Hartford ■ 860 236 6299
■ Closed Sun L; open Sun brunch
■ www.maxrestaurantgroup.com
Showmanlike presentation of the
raw-bar offerings sets the tone for
this polished, dressy seafood joint.

2 City Steam Brewery Cafe
MAP C4 ■ 942 Main St, Hartford
Great beers brewed on site, super
competent waitstaff, and good casual
American grub make this restaurant,
in a landmark building, a delight. It
even has a comedy club.

3 Toad's Place
MAP C5 ■ 300 York St,
New Haven
One of the state's biggest dance
floors and a sound system that could
rock a stadium make Toad's *the*
dance venue on a Saturday night.

4 Pastorale Bistro & Bar
MAP B4 ■ 223 Main St,
Salisbury ■ www.pastoralebistro.com
Lauded for its French bistro classics
made with locally grown ingredients,
this bistro and *boîte* in a 1760 Colonial
house boasts a sophisticated list of
cocktails and a good wine cellar.

5 Water Street Café
MAP E5 ■ 143 Water St,
Stonington
Locals favor Water Street for great
oysters at the raw bar, chilled white
wine, and live guitar music, but don't
overlook lively dishes like the lobster
spring rolls or warm duck salad.

6 @ the Corner
MAP B4 ■ 3 West St, Litchfield
This hip bakery (formerly The Blue
Bakery) makes cakes piled with
frosting and pies bursting with
fillings. It also serves good coffee
and espresso, and a selection of
soups, sandwiches, and salads.

7 MacDuff's Public House
MAP A6 ■ 99 Railroad Ave,
Greenwich
There's a certain amount of tartan
posturing in the decor of this
sophisticated Scottish-themed pub.
European soccer games often
dominate the TV over the bar.

8 The Loft Martini Lounge
MAP B6 ■ 97 Washington St,
S Norwalk
Connecticut's best martinis are all
you really need to know about The
Loft, which is so named for the
people-watching mezzanine up
a wrought-iron staircase.

9 The Cask Republic
MAP C5 ■ 179 Crown St,
New Haven
Craft beer is taken seriously here,
with more than 40 taps active at a
time. The long lists of Scotch and
Bourbon are augmented by local
crafts spirits. The menu includes
charcuterie, burgers, and desserts.

10 Wine Bar at the Griswold Inn
MAP D5 ■ 36 Main St, Essex
Mature cheeses and tapas-style
platters can be matched with at least
50 wines at this intimate bar, where
maritime art adorns the walls.

Places to Shop

 "The Avenue," Greenwich

MAP A6

Greenwich is the "platinum" town on Connecticut's Gold Coast, and Greenwich Avenue is packed with luxury boutiques that will feather the finest nest.

2 Guilford Art Center

MAP C5 ▪ 411 Church St, Guilford

The town green bustles each July with a juried exhibition of fine crafts. But this center promotes crafts year-round, with classes and a shop full of unique hand-crafted items.

3 Woodbury Pewter

MAP B5 ▪ 860 Main St S, Woodbury

You could well discover the perfect candlestick, bowl, or teapot at a discounted price at the factory outlet of this family-owned company, which was founded in 1952.

 The Shops at Mohegan Sun

MAP D5 ▪ 1 Mohegan Sun Blvd, Uncasville

Visitors who strike it rich at the gaming tables and slot machines will find plenty to tempt them to splash out on in the upscale shops of this casino complex.

Casino shopping at Mohegan Sun

5 Stamford

MAP A6 ▪ United House Wrecking: 535 Hope St, Stamford

Interior decorators scour the immense United House Wrecking for architectural salvage, lawn ornaments, or unusual furniture and accessories. If you're not driving a van, other shops in town stock smaller collectibles.

6 Olde Mistick Village

MAP D5 ▪ Coogan Blvd, Mystic

Lush gardens, a duck pond, and a waterwheel accent this quaint complex not far from Mystic Seaport (see p46). There's even an old-fashioned general store.

7 The Silo Store

MAP B5 ▪ 44 Upland Rd, New Milford

Musician Skitch Henderson and his wife left their farm to a trust. The couple loved fine food; the shop (in the farm's silo) features gourmet cookware and hosts cooking classes.

8 Chapel St, New Haven

MAP C5

Chapel Street skirts the edge of the Yale campus with shops catering to faculty and students alike. Look for designer clothing boutiques and bookstore cafés.

9 Putnam

MAP D4 ▪ Antiques Marketplace: 109 Main St

Setting up the Antiques Marketplace in an ex-department store breathed new life into this former mill town. If you can't find your collectible there, check the town's smaller shops.

10 Clinton Crossing Premium Outlets

MAP C5 ▪ 20-A Killingworth Turnpike, Clinton

Get up to 65 per cent off designer wear at over 70 stores, including DKNY, Calvin Klein, Kenneth Cole, and outlets for Saks Fifth Avenue and Barneys New York.

See map on pp94–5

🔟 Vermont

The majestic Green Mountains that cover Vermont compensate for the lack of a seacoast. Between the peaks stand high green meadows and deep, dark lakes, two of which are said to harbor sea serpents. Settled in the 1700s under conflicting land grants from New York and New Hampshire, Vermont was an independent republic from 1777, becoming the 14th US state in 1791. A rugged independence persists in Vermonters, who despite severe winter weather seem to be outdoors year-round, hiking, skiing, skating, sledding, cycling, kayaking, hunting, and fishing, sometimes against a brilliant background of fall leaves.

Skiing in Northeast Kingdom

AREA MAP OF VERMONT

Burlington

1	**Top 10 Sights** see pp107–9
1	**Restaurants** see p113
1	**The Best of the Rest** see p110
1	**Bars and Cafés** see p112
1	**Tastes of Vermont** see p111

Previous pages Jordan Pond in Acadia National Park, Maine

The breathtaking wilderness of the beautiful Green Mountains

1 Green Mountains

It would scarcely be an exaggeration to say that Vermont *is* the Green Mountains and vice versa, as this ancient range in the Appalachian chain touches almost every part of the state *(see pp26–7)*.

2 Brattleboro
MAP K6

Vermont's first permanent English settlement, Brattleboro flourished in the 19th century as a Connecticut River manufacturing town at the juncture of Vermont, Massachusetts, and New Hampshire. The town got a new lease on life in the 1960s as the counterculture capital of the upper Connecticut River Valley, and is known around the state for its stridently liberal politics. The thriving cultural community includes several galleries, a performing arts center, and a school of circus arts that is open to the general public.

3 Newport
MAP L5

Vermont's northernmost city is set at the southern edge of Lake Memphremagog, a body of water 27 miles (43 km) long that is shared with the province of Quebec. A glacial lake that was a saltwater inland sea at the end of the Laurentian glaciation, Memphremagog has long been rumored to hold a sea serpent akin to the Loch Ness Monster. Sightings of the elusive creature that locals call "Memphre" date to the 18th century. Take a stroll along the attractive waterfront and see if you can spy those watery coils from the safety of the shore.

4 Montpelier
MAP K3

For an iconic Vermont image, stop along State Street during foliage season to take a snapshot of the gold-domed State House backed by a hillside of red and flame-orange maple trees. The city was selected for state capital in 1805 because it lies at the geographic center of Vermont as well as in the main east-west pass through the Green Mountains. The highly regarded New England Culinary Institute guarantees that Montpelier eats well, especially at the school's NECI on Main *(see p113)*.

Vermont State House, Montpelier

ETHAN ALLEN

Vermont folk hero Ethan Allen (1738–89) led a militia called the Green Mountain Boys. He is hailed for rebuffing colonial governors and British troops alike in a quest for Vermont's independence. His capture of Fort Ticonderoga from British forces in 1775 played a key strategic role early in the American Revolution.

5 Grafton

MAP K6 ■ Plummer's Sugar House: 2866 Townshend Rd; 802 843 2207; www.plummerssugarhouse.com ■ Grafton Village Cheese Co: 533 Townshend Rd; 800 472 3866; www.graftonvillagecheese.com ■ Old Tavern: 92 Main St; 802 843 2231

Wealthy philanthropists saved this beautiful village in the 1960s by forming the Windham Foundation to restore its handsome buildings and revitalize commerce. Visit Plummer's Sugar House or the Grafton Village Cheese Co., or enjoy a delicious meal at the 200-year-old Old Tavern.

Verdant pastures of Shelburne Farms

6 Shelburne

MAP J3 ■ Vermont Wildflower Farm: 3488 Ethan Allen Hwy, Charlotte; 802 425 3641; open mid-May–mid-Sep: 10am–3:30pm Mon–Fri; www.vermontwildflowerfarm.com

Standing on high banks above Lake Champlain just south of Burlington, Shelburne is a village of magnificent dairy farms, not least among them the historic spread of Shelburne Farms (see p111). A locomotive, a steamship, and buildings crammed with folk art dot the rolling meadows of Shelburne Museum (see p41). South of town, just into Charlotte, the Vermont Wildflower Farm has over 350 species of flowering plants and trees on the grounds.

7 Northeast Kingdom

MAP L2

"Northeast Kingdom" refers to Essex, Orleans, and Caledonia counties in the state's northeast corner – an area sometimes referred to simply as "The Kingdom." In Vermont cultural shorthand, the term connotes both a rural, frontier toughness and an easy familiarity with the latest developments in the world of avant-garde performance art. With only two large communities, St. Johnsbury and Newport, it is one of the most rural parts of the state. The Northeast Kingdom is known above all for skiing, resplendent autumn foliage, and maple syrup.

8 Burlington

MAP J3

Settled shortly before the American Revolution, Burlington, unlike the rest of Vermont, takes its identity less from the Green Mountains than from the great inland sea of Lake Champlain. Burlington shipyards turned the mountain timber into trading vessels. Visitors can learn about the region's history on the Lake Champlain Cruise (see p60). Blessed with a handsome, largely 19th-century downtown, Burlington also enjoys a busy cultural life as a by-product of the presence of the state university.

Marketplace, downtown Burlington

Traditional houses, Woodstock

9 Woodstock and Quechee
MAP K5

It's little wonder that Woodstock is such a popular destination for weddings. With its broad town green, meticulously restored Federal and Victorian houses, covered bridge in the middle of town, and five churches boasting Paul Revere bells, it is the very picture of old-time Vermont. Even the Billings Farm (see p38) serves as a museum of Vermont rural life. Head east on Route 4 to see the vertigo-inspiring 165-ft (50-m) deep gorge carved by the Ottauquechee River.

10 St. Johnsbury
MAP L3 ▪ Athenaeum Gallery: 1171 Main St; 802 748 8291; open 10am–5:30pm Mon, Wed & Fri, 2–7pm Tue & Thu, 10am–3pm Sat; www.stjathenaeum.org

"St. J," as Vermonters call it, is both the hub of the state's Northeast Kingdom and the gateway between Vermont's Green Mountains and New Hampshire's White Mountains. When Thaddeus Fairbanks invented the platform scale in 1830, the town became his manufacturing center. The Fairbanks clan left its stamp on St. Johnsbury, donating both the Fairbanks Museum & Planetarium (see p110), and the Athenaeum, a library and gallery with magnificent landscape paintings.

A DAY IN ROBERT FROST COUNTRY

▶ MORNING

Robert Frost (1874–1963), the seminal poet of the New England countryside, spent 39 summers in the **Green Mountain National Forest** (see pp26–7). This easy-to-moderate day of hiking captures the poet and the landscape he loved. Start with pancakes and maple syrup at the **Rochester Café** (Rte 100, Rochester; 802 767 4302), at the same soda fountain where Frost used to eat, and have the café pack you a lunch. Drive west on Rte 125 to the **Robert Frost Interpretive Trail**, where you can read some of Frost's pithy verse and learn to identify native plants. Just east of the almost adjacent Robert Frost Wayside picnic area, a 5-minute walk on an unmarked dirt road will bring you to Frost's cabin at the **Homer Noble Farm**, maintained as he left it.

AFTERNOON

When the muse evaded Frost, he sought solace in the woods. For a hike, drive east on Rte 125 a short distance and turn left onto **Steam Mill Road**. A bit further on, park at the **Skylight Pond** trailhead. The path ascends the flank of Battell Mountain, crisscrossing the hillside through a forest of white birch, red oak, and hemlocks. Overgrown and tumbledown stone walls proclaim old boundary lines, as forest reclaims farmland. The moderate 45-minute climb ends on a ridge connecting to the legendary **Long Trail**. Turn left for a short hike to **Skyline Lodge**, a rustic shelter for hikers.

See map on p106 ←

The Best of the Rest

Enthralled child, Montshire Museum

1 Montshire Museum
MAP L4 ▪ 1 Montshire Rd, Norwich ▪ 802 649 2200 ▪ Open daily ▪ Adm ▪ www.montshire.org

This museum has outdoor trails and science exhibits that delight children.

2 Fairbanks Museum & Planetarium
MAP L3 ▪ 1302 Main St, St. Johnsbury ▪ 802 748 2372 ▪ Open daily ▪ Adm ▪ www.fairbanksmuseum.org

Vermont flora and fauna mingle with Philippine and Indian birds in this natural history museum.

3 President Calvin Coolidge State Historic Site
MAP K5 ▪ 3780 Rte 100 A, Plymouth ▪ 802 672 3773 ▪ Open daily late May–mid-Oct ▪ Adm ▪ www.historicvermont.org

The independent spirit of his home village inspired Coolidge (1872–1933). Today, much remains the same.

4 Robert Hull Fleming Museum
MAP J3 ▪ 61 Colchester Ave, Burlington ▪ 802 656 2090 ▪ Closed Mon; mid-Dec–mid-Jan; mid-Mar; Jul–Aug ▪ Adm ▪ www.uvm.edu/~fleming

Artifacts ranging from African masks and pre-Columbian pottery to medieval manuscripts and Andy Warhol prints are displayed here.

5 Bennington Museum & Grandma Moses Gallery
MAP J6 ▪ 75 Main St, Bennington ▪ 802 447 1571 ▪ Closed Jan; Wed ▪ Adm ▪ www.benningtonmuseum.org

Stop by and browse this major collection of work by folk artist Grandma Moses (1860–1961).

6 VTSSM
MAP K3 ▪ 1 S Main St, Stowe ▪ 802 253 9911 ▪ Closed Mon–Tue ▪ Donation ▪ www.vtssm.com

Vermont Ski and Snowboard Museum charts skiing in the state from the introduction of powered lifts in the 1930s to the present day.

7 Vermont Institute of Natural Science
MAP K5 ▪ 6565 Woodstock Rd, Rte 4, Quechee ▪ 802 359 5000 ▪ Adm ▪ www.vinsweb.org

Injured eagles, hawks, and other raptors, unable to return to the wild, get a second home here.

8 UVM Morgan Horse Farm
MAP J4 ▪ 74 Battell Dr, Weybridge ▪ 802 388 2011 ▪ Open daily May–Oct ▪ Adm ▪ www.uvm.edu/morgan

The graceful Morgan horse, one of the first US breeds, is bred here.

9 Vermont Covered Bridge Museum
MAP J6 ▪ Rte 9 at Gypsy Ln, Bennington ▪ 802 442 7158 ▪ Closed Tue ▪ Adm ▪ www.thebennington.org/covered-bridge

Come here to learn how Vermont's iconic bridges were constructed.

10 American Museum of Fly Fishing
MAP K6 ▪ 4104 Main St, Manchester ▪ 802 362 3300 ▪ Closed Sun–Mon ▪ Adm ▪ www.amff.com

Exhibits such as rods, reels, flies, and books tell the story of this most philosophical of outdoor pursuits.

Tastes of Vermont

1 Cold Hollow Cider Mill
MAP K3 ■ 3600 Waterbury-Stowe Rd, Rte 100, Waterbury Center ■ 802 244 8771 ■ Open daily ■ www.coldhollow.com

Drop by for freshly pressed cider. The store brims with Vermont specialties.

2 Lake Champlain Chocolates
MAP J3 ■ 750 Pine St, Burlington ■ 802 864 1808 ■ Factory tours: Mon–Fri ■ www.lakechamplain chocolates.com

Watch cream and butter being blended with fine chocolate to form the decadent bars and truffles sold here.

3 Magic Hat Brewery
MAP J3 ■ 5 Bartlett Bay Rd, S Burlington ■ 802 658 2739 ■ Open daily ■ www.magichat.net

Magic Hat's oddball brews include raspberry stout and honey ale.

Chocolates at Lake Champlain

4 Ben & Jerry's Ice Cream Factory
MAP K3 ■ Rte 100, Waterbury ■ 866 BJ TOURS ■ Open daily ■ Adm ■ www.benjerry.com

Vermont farms provide the rich milk for the super-premium ice creams and yogurts that are made here.

5 Crowley Cheese Co
MAP K5 ■ 14 Crowley Ln, Healdville ■ 802 259 2340 ■ Open Mon–Sat ■ www.crowleycheese-vermont.com

This is Vermont's oldest cheese factory (1882), noted for its prize-winning Colby cheese.

6 Shelburne Farms
MAP J3 ■ 1611 Harbor Rd, Shelburne ■ 802 985 8442 ■ Store open daily; tours May–Oct ■ Adm for tours ■ www.shelburnefarms.org

Milk from Brown Swiss cows is turned into cheddar at this farm overlooking Lake Champlain.

7 Maple Grove Farms Maple Museum and Gift Shop
MAP L3 ■ 1052 Portland St, St. Johnsbury ■ 802 748 5141 ■ Open Apr–May: Mon–Fri; Jun–Dec: daily ■ Adm ■ www.maplegrove.com

Learn how tree sap becomes a breakfast favorite. Then watch that maple syrup transformed into candies.

8 Lincoln Peak Winery
MAP J4 ■ 142 River Rd, New Haven ■ 802 388 7368 ■ Open late May–mid-Oct: 11am–5pm daily; mid-Oct–Dec: Wed–Sun; Jan–late May: Sat ■ www.lincolnpeak vineyard.com

The tasting room at Lincoln Peak offers some of the best wines made in the inhospitable northerly climate.

9 Vermont Country Store
MAP K5 ■ 657 Main St, Weston ■ 802 824 3184 ■ Open daily ■ www.vermontcountrystore.com

This emporium still has a pickle barrel and huge wedges of cheddar. Try its own Vermont Common Crackers.

10 Cabot Creamery
MAP L3 ■ 2878 Main St, Cabot ■ 800 837 4261 ■ Closed Sun Nov–May ■ Adm (for tour) ■ www.cabot cheese.com

Vermont's largest cheese producer stocks a wide range of dairy products.

Dairy items for sale, Cabot Creamery

See map on p106

Bars and Cafés

1 Higher Ground
MAP J3 ▪ 1214 Williston Rd, Burlington ▪ 802 253 4364 ▪ $

The state's premier music venue hosts an array of acts, ranging from chart-toppers to obscure indie bands. Three full-service bars keep the crowds fueled.

2 Drink
MAP J3 ▪ 135 St. Paul St, Burlington

This sophisticated northern Vermont bar offers splashy mojitos, cosmopolitans, and a selection of home-infused vodkas. Traditionalists may bypass the stylish lounge in favor of beer and televised sports at the bar.

3 McGrath's Irish Pub
MAP K5 ▪ Inn at Long Trail, 709 Rte 4, Sherburne Pass, Killington

Darts, Guinness on draft, and live music on weekends await the loyal following at this amiable pub.

Perfect Wife Restaurant

4 Perfect Wife Restaurant
MAP K6 ▪ 2594 Depot St, Manchester Center ▪ $

Judging by the menu, a "perfect wife" can cook a pot of chili or grill a steelhead trout. Live music on weekends brings in the local crowd.

5 Baba-a-Louis Bakery
MAP K5 ▪ 92 Rte 11 W, Chester

In addition to French baguettes and organic whole wheat loaves to take home, there's a lunch buffet that features sandwiches and soups.

Prohibition Pig

6 Prohibition Pig
MAP K3 ▪ 23 S Main St, Waterbury ▪ $

A friendly local hangout that whips up classic cocktails alongside Vermont's most acclaimed craft beers. Delicious barbecue fare and a gluten-free menu keep the patrons satisfied.

7 Maglianero
MAP J3 ▪ 47 Maple St, Burlington ▪ 802 861 3155 ▪ $

Outstanding expresso and a few treats, such as tenderloin flatbread with caramelized onions, are on offer at this coffee shop. A must-stop for tea fans, too.

8 Jasper Murdock's Alehouse
MAP L4 ▪ 325 Main St, Norwich

This cozy pub brews its own English-style ales. It attracts large numbers of students from nearby Dartmouth College, as well as local ski buffs.

9 Matterhorn
MAP K3 ▪ 4969 Mountain Rd, Stowe

The first bar south of Stowe's Mount Mansfield, the Matterhorn is party central after a day of skiing. Escape the hubbub in the martini bar.

10 Mocha Joe's Café
MAP K6 ▪ 82 Main St, Brattleboro

Artists, musicians, and all self-respecting Brattleboro Bohemians get caffeinated at this roaster café known for its winter maple lattes and summer limeade.

Restaurants

1 Inn at Shelburne Farms Restaurant

MAP J3 ■ 1611 Harbor Rd, Shelburne ■ 802 985 8498 ■ Open mid-May–mid-Oct, B and D daily, Sun brunch ■ $$

This elegant dining room makes the most of northern Vermont's short but high-grade harvest, from early lettuces to fall apples.

2 Hen of the Wood

MAP K3 ■ 92 Stowe St, Waterbury ■ 802 244 7300 ■ Closed L, Sun–Mon ■ $$

Plates here embody the essence of gastronomic Vermont: local meats, seasonal farm vegetables, foraged foods, and exquisite cheeses.

3 Farmhouse Tap & Grill

MAP J3 ■ 160 Bank St, Burlington ■ 802 859 0888 ■ Open L & D daily ■ $$

Gourmet burgers, craft beer, and dinner plates laden with Vermont farm produce make Farmhouse a local favorite.

4 Cafe Provence

MAP K4 ■ 111 Center St, Brandon ■ 802 247 9997 ■ Closed Mon ■ $$

The Provençal chef uses Vermont produce to create authentic country French food served in an intimate village bistro.

5 The Mill at Simon Pearce

MAP K5 ■ 1760 Quechee Main St, Quechee ■ 802 295 1470 ■ Closed Sun L; open Sun brunch ■ $$

Savor the riverside location, superb food, and fine wine. Pearce, a famed glass artist, has a studio on site.

6 Kitchen Table Bistro

MAP K3 ■ 1840 W Main St, Richmond ■ 802 434 8686 ■ Closed L, Sun & Mon D ■ $$

This cozy bistro operated by two graduates of the New England Culinary Institute has a strong northern-French accent. Try the maple-smoked pork and braised kale.

7 NECI on Main

MAP K3 ■ 118 Main St, Montpelier ■ 802 223 3188 ■ Closed Mon; open Sat & Sun brunch ■ $

Student chefs at the New England Culinary Institute train here.

Scallops served at NECI on Main

8 Starry Night Café

MAP J3 ■ 5371 Rte 7, Ferrisburg ■ 802 877 6316 ■ Closed L, Mon & Tue D ■ $$

Dining here in a covered bridge or a former cider house is as magical as the restaurant name. Hearty American food is mostly raised or grown locally.

9 American Flatbread

MAP J4 ■ 137 Maple St, Middlebury ■ 802 388 3300 ■ Closed L, Sun–Thu; D, Sun–Mon ■ $

This wildly popular eatery churns out gourmet pizzas and salads made with organic, Vermont-raised ingredients.

10 The Inn at Weathersfield

MAP K5 ■ 1342 Rte 106, Perkinsville ■ 802 263 9217 ■ Closed L, Mon–Wed D ■ $$

Inventive chefs here might pair pork loin and scallops with capers, or pumpkin soup with local blue cheese.

See map on p106

🔟 New Hampshire

The aptly nicknamed Granite State is a thick wedge of rock between two great rivers – the Connecticut on the west and the Piscataqua on the east. Its initial settlements in the 1620s were strictly coastal, but within a generation, explorers had ventured deep into its woods for furs and timber. Despite the rugged topography, many of the villages in the White Mountains were well established by the time of the American Revolution. Most residents live along the southern edge of the state, often driving down to Massachusetts for employment. Northern New Hampshire remains almost untracked forest. American scenic tourism began in the White Mountains in the 1820s, and those peaks and the villages on their flanks remain major vacation destinations. New Hampshire also boasts a chain of alpine lakes and a lively seacoast, where vacationers from as far away as Montreal flock to the shore.

The church in Keene

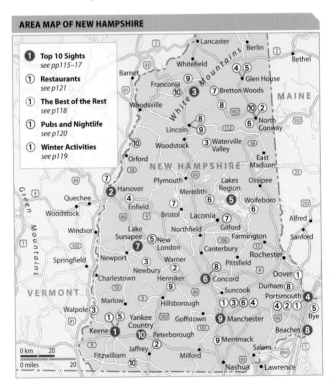

AREA MAP OF NEW HAMPSHIRE

1 **Top 10 Sights**
see pp115–17

1 **Restaurants**
see p121

1 **The Best of the Rest**
see p118

1 **Pubs and Nightlife**
see p120

1 **Winter Activities**
see p119

1 Keene
MAP L6

At 132 ft (40 m) wide for most of its length, Keene's attractive Main Street is easily the widest in New England. This shire town has a lively mix of old-time shops and art galleries, as well as the good bars and cafés you'd expect in a college community. At its heart stands the pretty United Church of Christ with its soaring white steeple.

2 Hanover
MAP L4 ■ Ledyard Canoe Club of DOC: Ledyard Bridge; 603 643 6709; open May–Oct; call for availability; adm

It's hardly a bad thing, but Dartmouth College utterly overwhelms the rest of Hanover. The town green and the college green are one and the same, and the shopping district clearly favors the tastes of young scholars and their well-heeled parents. But Dartmouth holds many riches, even for the visitor just passing through. Not least among them are the art treasures of the Hood Museum of Art *(see p43)* – closed until 2019 for expansion. Hanover sits on the Connecticut River and is popular with canoeists. Most recreational programs of the Dartmouth Outing Club, including boat rentals, are open to non-students as well.

3 White Mountains
The White Mountains have a special place in American history. When early 19th-century poets,

White Mountains, a hub for hikers

philosophers, and theologians sought inspiration, they made a pilgrimage to these majestic hills to experience the sublime rising peaks and plunging glens *(see pp20–21)*.

4 Portsmouth
MAP N6

Portsmouth was New Hampshire's first English community, settled at the mouth of the Piscataqua River in 1623. Plentiful timber and a deep harbor made it a natural for ship-building, and from 1780 to 1870 its merchant traders grew rich. Walk through the handsome squares of the Colonial settlement to see some of New England's finest town mansions, and to breathe the salt air that has always been Portsmouth's life-blood. The historic houses and period furnishings of Strawbery Banke *(see p38)* relate the city's four-century domestic history.

Portsmouth, on the Piscataqua River

Small islands dotting the water in New Hampshire's Lakes Region

⑤ Lakes Region

Vast lakes and small ponds form a stunning watery belt across New Hampshire's midriff. Seek solitude among the loons on a remote cove, or party all night on Weirs Beach *(see pp30–31)*.

⑥ Concord

MAP M5 ■ New Hampshire Historical Society: 30 Park St; 603 228 6688; open 9:30am–5pm Tue–Sat, noon–5pm Sun; adm; www. nhhistory.org

The state capital Concord is a serene little town steeped in history. Its handsome 1819 State House is one of the country's oldest. The celebrated Concord stagecoaches that helped to open up the American West were manufactured here; Mark Twain memorably described one as being "like a cradle on wheels." The city's most famous modern resident was schoolteacher Christa McAuliffe (1948–86), who died aboard the *Challenger* space shuttle. Her dedication to science education is honored at the McAuliffe-Shepard Discovery Center *(see p62)*.

State House, Concord

⑦ Lake Sunapee

MAP L5 ■ Sunapee Cruises: 1 Lake Ave, Sunapee; 603 938 6465; open late May–mid-Oct; adm; www. mvkearsarge.com

This alpine lake – whose name, meaning "wild goose waters," is of American-Indian origin – was a Victorian resort where vacationers stepped off the train onto steamboats to be delivered to their grand lakefront hotels. The hotels are gone, but private cottages ring the lake, and the harbors of Sunapee and Newbury are busy spots in the summer, with free outdoor concerts and bustling restaurants. Take a scenic cruise on the lake, or have a dinner cruise on a steamboat.

⑧ Beaches

MAP N6

New Hampshire's brief stretch of coastline is more rock than sand, with rugged promontories and rock jetties protecting its fishing harbors. The coast is also punctuated by swaths of coarse brown sand. Jenness State Beach and Wallis Sands State Beach in Rye, and North Beach in Hampton, have the best-maintained facilities and gentlest swimming. Hampton Beach *(see p52)* is by far the most popular.

⑨ Manchester

MAP M6

The largest city in northern New England, Manchester rose and fell with the Amoskeag Mill. From humble beginnings in 1809 on the east bank of the Merrimack River, the

LIVE FREE OR DIE

Some visitors might imagine that the state motto proclaimed on license plates refers to New Hampshire's lack of sales and income taxes, but in fact it originated with a toast that the state's Revolutionary War hero, General John Stark, gave by letter to an 1809 reunion of veterans of the Battle of Bennington, when poor health prevented him from attending: "Live free or die: death is not the worst of evils."

town grew into the world's largest cotton-mill complex by the dawn of the 20th century. The textile era has long since ended here, but the hulking brick mills have been transformed into a complex of restaurants, college classrooms, offices, and apartments. The city's comprehensive Currier Museum of Art (see p40) is the state's premier art museum.

Peterborough, stunning in the fall

⑩ Yankee Country
MAP L6

Yankee Publishing, which produces both *Yankee Magazine* and the *Old Farmer's Almanac*, is based in Dublin. The homespun village and its neighboring towns of Peterborough and Jaffrey epitomize the gentle New England countryside. The region was a popular resort area in the late 19th century, and all three villages have long served as staging grounds for people preparing to climb nearby Mount Monadnock (see p61), said to be the second most-climbed peak in the world after Japan's Mount Fuji.

▶ MORNING

Before you begin the 35-mile (56-km) drive from **Lincoln** to **Conway** (see pp20–21), stop at **Half Baked & Fully Brewed** (187 Main St, Lincoln) for picnic fixings. After a gentle 11-mile (18-km) rise, you'll climb through steep switchbacks for 4 miles (6 km) to the **Graham Wangan Ground Overlook** for jaw-dropping mountain views. As the road twists and turns for another 6 miles (10 km), watch for a right turn into the trailhead to **Sabbaday Falls**. A short walk through dense, pine-scented woods brings you to the waterfall, which makes a wonderfully dramatic 90-degree dogleg as it tumbles down a mountain. The **Rocky Gorge Scenic Area**, a further 4 miles (6 km) east, is a geological wonder. Cross a bridge to follow a short trail to **Falls Pond**, where fishermen cast for trout.

AFTERNOON

Another 3 miles (5 km) east, spread your food on a picnic table at **Lower Falls**, overlooking the boulder-strewn **Swift River**. The green pools below the largest boulders make cool summer swimming holes. In the fall, photographers scramble across the boulders trying to capture the intense red and yellow foliage. From the Falls, it's only a short drive to the **Albany Covered Bridge** (see p61). The weathered 120-ft (37-m) span is a favorite with photographers and you'll surely want a shot to remember your journey. From the bridge, it's about 7 fairly flat miles (11 km) to the end of the "Kanc" in Conway.

See map on p114

The Best of the Rest

1 Children's Museum of New Hampshire
MAP N5 ▪ 6 Washington St, Dover ▪ 603 742 2002 ▪ Closed Mon except in summer and school vacations ▪ Adm ▪ www.childrens-museum.org

A yellow submarine and an interactive sound sculpture are two of the imaginative exhibits here.

2 Mount Kearsarge Indian Museum
MAP L5 ▪ 18 Highlawn Rd, Warner ▪ 603 456 2600 ▪ Open May–Oct: daily ▪ Adm ▪ www.indianmuseum.org

Exhibit, Mount Kearsage Indian Museum

Admire intricate craftwork and learn how plants were used for food and medicine at this fascinating museum.

3 Mount Sunapee State Park
MAP L5 ▪ 86 Beach Access Rd, Newbury ▪ 603 763 5561 (park); 603 763 3500 (ski resort) ▪ Open late May–mid-Sep (beach); late Nov–mid-Apr (ski resort) ▪ Adm ▪ www.nhstateparks.org

This state park has a pristine lake for swimming, fishing, and boating, as well as 65 ski trails in winter.

4 Enfield Shaker Museum
MAP L5 ▪ 447 Rte 4A, Enfield ▪ 603 632 4346 ▪ Open daily ▪ Adm ▪ www.shakermuseum.org

Like the furniture and tools displayed inside, the Great Stone Dwelling has an austere grace.

Enfield Shaker Museum

5 Odiorne Point State Park
MAP N6 ▪ Rte 1A, Rye ▪ 603 436 7406 ▪ Open year-round daily ▪ Adm ▪ www.nhstateparks.org

Tidal pools, pebble beaches, and marshlands surround the site of the state's first English settlement.

6 Wright Museum
MAP M5 ▪ 77 Center St, Wolfeboro ▪ 603 569 1212 ▪ Open May–Oct ▪ Adm ▪ www.wrightmuseum.org

This museum highlights the World War II efforts of US services and their home-front sacrifices.

7 Wellington State Park
MAP L5 ▪ 614 W Shore Rd, Bristol ▪ 603 744 2197 ▪ Open mid-May–mid-Oct: Sat–Sun (mid-Jun–Aug: daily) ▪ Adm ▪ www.nhstateparks.org

The swimming beach on Newfound Lake is a summer favorite. Hike the nature trails in the fall for the foliage.

8 Crawford Notch State Park
MAP M4 ▪ 1464 Rte 302, Hart's Location ▪ 603 374 2272 ▪ Open daily ▪ Adm ▪ www.nhstateparks.org

This vast wilderness is a hiker's paradise. Climb 2,804-ft (855-m) Mount Willard for great views.

9 Budweiser Brewery Experience
MAP M6 ▪ 221 Daniel Webster Hwy, Merrimack ▪ 603 595 1202 ▪ Closed Jan–May: Tue–Wed ▪ www.budweisertours.com

This informative brewery tour concludes with a tasting for over 21s.

10 Rhododendron State Park
MAP L6 ▪ 424 Rockwood Pond Rd, Fitzwilliam ▪ 603 532 8862 ▪ Open year-round ▪ www.nhstateparks.org

Immerse yourself in the color and aroma of the towering rhododendrons that bloom here in June and July.

Winter Activities

1 **Manchester Monarchs**
MAP M6 ■ 555 Elm St, Manchester ■ 603 626 7825 ■ Open Oct–Apr ■ Adm ■ www.manchester monarchs.com
A family-friendly atmosphere underscores the games of this American Hockey League affiliate of the Los Angeles Kings.

2 **Outdoor Skating**
MAP M4 ■ Schouler Park, Main St, North Conway ■ Open Dec–Mar
Low temperatures guarantee a long season of outdoor skating at Schouler Park rink in this picturesque village.

3 **Nordic Skiing**
MAP M4 ■ Waterville Valley Resort, 1 Ski Area Rd, Waterville Valley ■ 603 236 4666 ■ Open Dec–Mar ■ Adm ■ www.waterville.com
Glide along scenic trails at the edge of the White Mountain National Forest.

4 **SnowCoach**
MAP M3 ■ Great Glen Trails, 1 Mt Washington Auto Rd, Gorham ■ 603 466 2333 ■ Open Dec–Mar: daily ■ Adm ■ www.mtwashington autoroad.com
This special vehicle carries passengers above the treeline on Mt Washington Auto Road for winter vistas.

5 **Snow Tubing**
MAP M3 ■ Great Glen Trails, 1 Mt Washington Auto Rd, Gorham ■ 603 466 2333 ■ Open Dec–Mar: daily ■ Adm ■ www.greatglentrails.com
For old-fashioned fun, climb a snow-covered hill and then whiz back down on a cushy, oversized inner tube.

6 **Horse-drawn Sleigh Rides**
MAP M4 ■ Farm by the River, 2555 West Side Rd, North Conway ■ 603 356 6640 ■ Open Dec–Feb: daily ■ Adm ■ www.farmbytheriver.com
Large sleighs depart from the stables several times daily. For romance, go for the intimate Victorian option.

7 **Dog Sledding**
MAP M3 ■ Mount Washington Resort, Rte 302, Bretton Woods ■ 603 278 1000 ■ Open Dec–Apr: Thu–Sun ■ Adm ■ www.mount washingtonresort.com
Alaskan huskies set off into the forested hills of Bretton Woods on trips of 20 minutes to an hour, led by experienced guides.

8 **Snowmobiling**
MAP L4 ■ SledVentures, 514 US Rte 3, Lincoln ■ 603 238 2571 ■ Open Nov–Mar ■ Adm ■ www. nhsledventures.com
Marvel at the hushed beauty of New Hampshire's snow-clad mountains in winter on a guided snowmobile tour.

Snowmobiling in the mountains

9 **Alpine Skiing**
MAP L/M 3–4
Thanks to the White Mountains, New Hampshire has a multitude of top-class alpine ski runs and all are easily reached via Rte 16 or 1-91.

10 **New England Ski Museum**
MAP L3 ■ Exit 34B I-93/Franconia Notch Parkway, Franconia ■ 603 823 7177 ■ Open late May–Mar: daily ■ www.skimuseum.org
The first aerial ski tramway in the US opened on Cannon Mountain in 1938. This is therefore a fitting location for this ski museum that traces the development of the sport from its roots to more modern times.

See map on p114

Pubs and Nightlife

 Elm City Brewing
MAP L6 ▪ Colony Mill Marketplace, 222 West St, Keene
The four-beer sampler offers a taste of the ales, porters, and stouts brewed in this 19th-century former woolen mill. Cozy booths make it ideal for conversation.

 Harlow's Pub
MAP L6 ▪ 3 School St, Peterborough
Visit this relaxed venue on Monday nights for a bluegrass jam; or try weekends, when it might be rock and blues, reggae, or even gypsy jazz.

3 **Strange Brew Tavern**
MAP M6 ▪ 88 Market St, Manchester
This friendly, bustling tavern serves a wide range of local brews along with an extensive menu of familiar pub grub. Local bands perform most nights.

4 **The Press Room**
MAP N6 ▪ 77 Daniel St, Portsmouth
Still going strong after three decades, this pub features live jazz from Sunday to Tuesday. The rest of the week might bring Celtic music and sea shanties, blues, soul, folk, or even poetry.

5 **Flying Goose Brew Pub**
MAP L5 ▪ 40 Andover Rd, New London
With a schedule of live music, "the Goose" lures regulars and travelers alike for hearty traditional food, malty ales made on the premises, and lively conversation.

 The Shaskeen
MAP M6 ▪ 909 Elm St, Manchester
This atmospheric pub was founded by two Irish musicians who put equal effort both into the nightly schedule of traditional Irish music and the classic Irish fare.

 Patrick's Pub & Eatery
MAP M5 ▪ 18 Weirs Rd, Gilford
Dueling pianos, open mic nights, and Saturday sessions of rotating musical styles create a lively atmosphere at Patrick's. Pints of Guinness complement the Irish-themed menu.

 Barley House
MAP M5 ▪ 132 N Main St, Concord
With a dozen fine imported and locally brewed beers on tap and a wood-paneled pub room, the Barley House feels more like a private club than a public bar.

9 **Woodstock Inn Station & Brewery**
MAP L4 ▪ 135 Main St, North Woodstock
English malts and international hops yield a range of outstanding ales geared for outdoors enthusiasts.

Roaring fire at the Woodstock Inn

10 **Moat Mountain Smoke House & Brewing Co**
MAP M4 ▪ 3378 White Mountain Hwy, Rte 16, North Conway
This ski-country restaurant takes barbecue seriously. The brisket is Texas dry rub, the pork comes Carolina-style (vinegar doused), and ribs come St. Louis-style. Match them all with the caramel brown ale.

Restaurants

1 Ristorante Massimo

MAP N6 ■ 59 Penhallow St, Portsmouth ■ 603 436 4000 ■ Closed L, Sun ■ $$

Sophisticated, largely northern Italian dishes make great use of New England seafood, especially lobster from local waters. The romantic dining room is set in an authentic Federal-era custom house.

2 Black Trumpet Bistro

MAP N6 ■ 29 Ceres St, Portsmouth ■ 603 431 0887 ■ Closed L ■ $$

The chef-owner transforms local seafood and produce into lusty American bistro dishes.

3 The Restaurant at Burdick's

MAP K6 ■ 47 Main St, Walpole ■ 603 756 9058 ■ Closed Mon, D Sun ■ $$$

Casual country French dining at this bistro complements the artisanal chocolates sold in the adjoining room.

4 Cotton

MAP M6 ■ 75 Arms St, Manchester ■ 603 622 5488 ■ Closed Sat–Sun L ■ $

Start with New Hampshire's best martini, then order from the menu of updated comfort food – meatloaf and mash, steak salad, buttermilk-fried chicken – in this seriously hip spot.

5 Luca's Mediterranean Café

MAP L6 ■ 10 Central Sq, Keene ■ 603 358 3335 ■ Closed Apr–Dec: Sat–Sun L; Jan–Mar: Sun ■ $

Northern Italian cuisine reigns at this casual but classy trattoria, although specials may be from North Africa and the eastern Mediterranean.

6 Hart's Turkey Farm Restaurant

MAP M5 ■ 233 Daniel Webster Hwy, Rtes 3 & 104, Meredith ■ 603 279 6212 ■ $

It's Thanksgiving every day at this family restaurant specializing in roast turkey dinners with all the fixings. You can also get your gobbler as a fricassee or with pasta.

Traditional inn atmosphere, Pine

7 Pine

MAP L4 ■ 2 S Main St, Hanover ■ 603 646 8000 ■ $$

At the venerable inn that serves as the center of Dartmouth College's social scene, Pine serves farm-to-table fare with local ingredients.

8 Three Chimneys Inn

MAP N6 ■ 17 Newmarket Rd, Durham ■ 603 868 7800 ■ Closed Sun–Mon L ■ $$

French country cooking is given a strong American accent here.

9 Colby Hill Inn

MAP L5 ■ 3 The Oaks, Henniker ■ 603 428 3281 ■ Closed L; Sun brunch ■ $$

Located in a romantic country setting, Colby Hill offers stately dining on classic New England dishes.

10 Ariana's Restaurant

MAP L4 ■ 1322 NH-10, Orford ■ 603 353 4405 ■ Closed Sun, Tue–Wed ■ $

Outstanding farm-to-fork restaurant on a farm down the road from an artisanal cheesemaker. American fare.

See map on p114 ⟵

🔟 Maine

Larger than New Hampshire, Connecticut, Rhode Island, and Vermont combined, Maine is New England on a grand scale. With a coast that wriggles around peninsulas and into harbors for an astonishing 5,500 miles (8,850 km) between Kittery and Calais, there's plenty to see without abandoning the smell of salt air. Turn off Route 1 down any peninsula, and you enter a world of scenic vistas and small villages, with a lobster harbor at the tip. Beaches stretch for miles along Maine's south coast. A province of Massachusetts from 1652 to 1820, Maine was famous well into the 20th century for harvesting timber and building tall ships. Even today, the state's windjammer fleet is one of the world's largest.

The Maine moose

AREA MAP OF MAINE

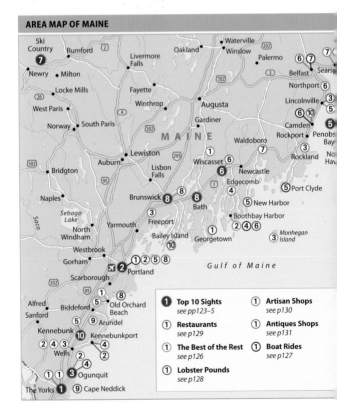

1 Top 10 Sights *see pp123–5*	**1** Artisan Shops *see p130*
1 Restaurants *see p129*	**1** Antiques Shops *see p131*
1 The Best of the Rest *see p126*	**1** Boat Rides *see p127*
1 Lobster Pounds *see p128*	

The 41-ft (12-m) tall Nubble Light lighthouse, built in 1879 at Cape Neddick

1 The Yorks

MAP N5, N6 ■ Museums of Old York: 3 Lindsay Rd; 207 363 1756; open late May–early Sep: 10am–5pm Tue–Sat, 1–5pm Sun (early Sep–mid-Oct: closed Tue–Wed); adm; www.oldyork.org

York has two very different faces: the historical York Village and the brassy summer playground of York Beach. Maine's first successful European settlement, York was founded in 1634; the Old York Historical Society chronicles local history. Long Sands and Short Sands swimming beaches are the main draws at York Beach, which also has a carousel and arcade. Drive to the end of Cape Neddick to see iconic Nubble Light.

Boats in the harbor at Portland

2 Portland and Casco Bay

Maine's largest community has the cultural advantages of a mid-sized city and all the natural beauty of a handsome, well-protected bay. The once-bedraggled maritime area has been reborn in the animated Old Port (see pp28–9).

3 Ogunquit

MAP N5

Plein air painters discovered Ogunquit in the 1890s, and visitors have been seeing beauty at every turn since. Picturesque Perkins Cove bristles with art galleries, souvenir shops, and seafood shacks. Marginal Way, a short trail over a rocky headland north of the cove, is lined with profusely blooming beach roses. The path exits onto Ogunquit Beach (see p53).

Mount Desert Island overlooking the waters of Frenchmen Bay

4 Mount Desert Island

French explorer Samuel de Champlain pinned the name *Ile des Monts Deserts* on this large island in 1604, and "island of bare mountains" has stuck ever since. The rocky balds that Champlain observed are prized among hikers and climbers in Acadia National Park (see pp14–15).

Yachts in serene Penobscot Bay

5 Penobscot Bay
MAP Q3

The west coast of Penobscot Bay is Maine's best-kept secret, although most of the state's windjammers (see p56) anchor in Rockland and Camden. Rockland is Maine's lobster capital and home of the treasured Farnsworth Art Museum (see p45); Camden has a beautiful harbor – a yacht-filled silver bowl at the foot of a mountain; Belfast is a community where artisans set the tone.

6 Wiscasset
MAP P4

Even simply driving through, you'll have plenty of time to contemplate Wiscasset's self-description as "the prettiest village in Maine" because the narrow bridge across the Sheepscot River backs traffic up in midsummer. Better to park and walk around this stunning village where adept 18th- and 19th-century ship-wrights turned their talents to build-ing houses for sea captains (see p48).

7 Ski Country
MAP N2

Moist air masses sweeping up the eastern seaboard meet the icy jet stream bringing Arctic air off the Canadian shield in northwest Maine, just east of the White Mountains. The result is massive dumps of snow that guarantee the peaks around Bethel, Newry, Kingfield, and Jackman will be buried in the white gold that skiers crave. In the summertime, long green meadows are transformed into championship golf courses.

8 Bath and Brunswick
MAP P4

Nearly half the US ocean-going sailing vessels launched in the late 19th century went down the ways from Bath shipyards – a history

---

THE MAINE MOOSE

The official state animal, the moose (*Alces alces*) is found all over Maine, with the greatest concentrations near Moosehead and Rangeley lakes. They often cross roads at dawn and dusk, so take special care driving through swampy areas. An 800-lb (363-kg) gentle giant makes a considerable impact in a collision.

detailed at the Maine Maritime Museum *(see p46)*. Nearby Brunswick is better known for making scholars than ships. Bowdoin College educated authors Nathaniel Hawthorne and Henry Wadsworth Longfellow, as well as intrepid Arctic explorers Robert Peary and Donald MacMillan. The college's Peary-MacMillan Arctic Museum *(see p42)* displays artifacts and images from their expeditions.

⑨ Moosehead Lake
MAP P1 ■ Visitor center: 480 Moosehead Lake Rd, Greenville; 207 695 2702; open late May–mid-Oct: 10am–4pm daily (closed Sun & Mon in off-season; www.mooseheadlake.org

The largest body of water contained within a single New England state, from the air, the lake resembles the antlers of a moose, and if you take a seaplane tour, you'll almost certainly see some of these impressive animals out for a swim. The lake is known for hunting, fishing, and winter snowmobiling, but photographic moose safaris are increasingly popular. Inquire at Greenville's visitor center.

⑩ Kennebunk
MAP N5 ■ Brick Store Museum: 117 Main St, Kennebunk; 207 985 4802; open 10am–4:30pm Tue–Fri, 10am–1pm Sat; adm; www.brickstoremuseum.org

The town of Kennebunk developed two distinct villages: Kennebunk on the river, and Kennebunkport where the river meets the ocean. Once a shipbuilding center, Kennebunk has now become principally a community of summer vacation homes. Visit the Brick Store Museum for exhibits on the town's cultural and historic heritage. Then head to Dock Square in Kennebunkport to peruse the boutiques and galleries.

Beach at Kennebunk

A DAY'S DRIVE IN WYETH COUNTRY

▶ MORNING

The rocky Maine coast has entranced many painters, but Andrew Wyeth (1917–2009) was among the few to chart the quiet country life of the saltwater farms. This drive shows you Maine through Wyeth's eyes. From Rte 1 in **Waldoboro**, turn south toward the village of **Friendship**, famed for its namesake sloop. You'll see lots of them in the harbor before continuing north toward **Cushing**. The **Olson House** was made famous in Wyeth's "Christina's World" (1948), and it looks little changed since Wyeth painted it. Continue north to Rte 1, passing through handsome **Thomaston**, and turn right at High St (Rte 131). Enjoy stunning vistas as you drive to **Port Clyde** at the tip of the peninsula, where the Monhegan Island *(see p50)* ferry departs.

AFTERNOON

North of the harbor, look for signs to **Marshall Point Lighthouse Museum**. The light was automated in 1971; the former keeper's house is a local history museum *(see p51)*. Head north again toward **Tenants Harbor** for dockside lobster at **Cod End** (Commercial St). Continue north to Rockland, to visit the **Maine Lighthouse Museum** *(see p47)*, and spend time at the **Farnsworth Art Museum** *(see p45)* enjoying art by three generations of Wyeth painters along with the work of modernist Louise Nevelson, who grew up in Rockland.

See map on pp122–3

The Best of the Rest

 Deer Isle and Stonington
MAP Q3

Artists and fishermen seem to flock together in Maine. The Haystack Mountain School of Crafts made Deer Isle famous years ago, while the lobster boats still tend to out-number pleasure craft in the striking harbor at Stonington.

2 Boothbay Harbor
MAP P4

Regarded by many as the boating capital of midcoast Maine, this picturesque harbor is a great spot to go on a whale-watching trip, kayak excursion, or pleasure cruise.

 Monhegan Island
MAP Q4

Birders and hikers flock to the rocky cliffs of this offshore art colony every summer. After the summer tourists leave, the lobster fishermen return for the profitable winter season.

4 Castine and Blue Hill
MAP Q3, R3

A drive down a single peninsula takes you to two great towns: art-minded Blue Hill, with its excellent pottery studios; and Castine, with its rich Colonial heritage and the Maine Maritime Academy.

5 Old Orchard Beach
MAP N5

This sandy beach, with its gentle surf, is the perfect place for swimming. Kids love the amusement park rides, the waterslide, and the pier with its fast food vendors and games of skill.

 Lubec and Campobello Island
MAP R2 ■ West Quoddy Head Light Visitor Center: 973 S Lubec Rd ■ 207 733 2180 ■ Open late May–mid-Oct: daily ■ www.westquoddy.com

America's first sunrise strikes the barber-pole lighthouse at West Quoddy Head in Lubec. A bridge leads to Campobello Island, where Franklin Roosevelt summered.

7 Bangor
MAP Q2

Fine mansions dot this Penobscot River town, once the world's timber capital and today a jumping-off point to the northern wilderness.

8 Baxter State Park
MAP Y5 ■ 64 Balsam Dr, Millinocket (office) ■ 207 723 5140 ■ Closed Sat–Sun mid-Oct–late May ■ www.baxterstateparkauthority.com

Test your mettle by scaling 5,267-ft (1,605-m) Mount Katahdin, set in 327 sq miles (848 sq km) of pristine forest.

9 Rangeley Lake Region
MAP N2

Spruce- and hemlock-clad peaks rise with robust grace from a plateau splashed with 112 lakes and ponds – an outdoors enthusiast's paradise.

10 Allagash Wilderness
MAP Y4–5 ■ Maine Bureau of Parks & Lands: 106 Hogan Rd, Bangor ■ 207 941 4014

Forever wild, the Allagash is a legendary system of rivers and lakes where the trout (and the mosquitoes) are bigger than anywhere else.

Old Orchard Beach

Boat Rides

1 Casco Bay Lines
 MAP N4 ■ 56 Commercial St, Portland ■ 207 774 7871 ■ Ferry year-round; some cruises summer only ■ Adm ■ www.cascobaylines.com

Sunrise, sunset, or moonlight cruises on the oldest ferry service in the US.

2 Three Rivers Whitewater
MAP P1 ■ 2265 Rte 201, West Forks ■ 207 663 2104 ■ Open May–Oct ■ Adm ■ Minimum age 10 ■ www.threeriverswhitewater.com

Hold on tight as your guide negotiates the thrilling waves and rapids on this adrenaline-filled rafting trip down the Kennebec River in Maine.

3 Bold Coast Charter Company
MAP R2 ■ Cutler Harbor ■ Open Jun–mid-Aug ■ Adm ■ Reservations essential ■ www.boldcoast.com

About 3,000 endangered puffins gather on Machias Seal Island. Bold Coast offers the only sightseeing trips for bird-watchers and photographers.

4 Cap'n Fish's Whale Watch
MAP P4 ■ 1 Wharf St, Boothbay Harbor ■ 207 633 3244 ■ Open late May–mid-Oct ■ Adm ■ www.whaleme.com

A shipboard naturalist will help you identify migrating whales. You might spot seals, porpoises, and dolphins.

5 Monhegan Boat Line
MAP Q4 ■ Port Clyde ■ 207 372 8848 ■ Closed Sun in winter ■ Adm ■ www.monheganboat.com

Drift past lobster boats on the trip out from Port Clyde to Monhegan Island, or opt for a cruise past the Muscongus Bay lighthouses.

6 Schooner Appledore
MAP Q3 ■ Bayview Landing, Camden ■ 207 236 8353 ■ Open Jun–Oct ■ Adm ■ www.appledore2.com

Get your sea legs with day sails around Penobscot Bay.

7 Maine Daysail
MAP Q3 ■ Thompson's Wharf, Belfast ■ 207 619 0654 ■ Open mid-Jun–early Oct ■ Adm ■ www.mainedaysail.com

Sail aboard the beautiful National Historic Landmark pilot schooner *Timberwind*. Day sails and sunset cruises out of Belfast explore the stunning midcoast Maine scenery.

SS *Katahdin* on Moosehead Lake

8 SS Katahdin
MAP P1 ■ 12 Lily Bay Rd, Greenville ■ 207 695 2716 ■ Open late Jun–mid-Oct ■ Adm ■ www.katahdincruises.com

Moosehead Lake is stunning during the fall foliage and there can be no better way to survey the scene than aboard the gloriously preserved SS *Katahdin*, a 1914 steamboat.

9 Downeast Windjammer Cruises
MAP R3 ■ Bar Harbor Inn Pier, Bar Harbor ■ 207 288 4585 ■ Open May–Oct ■ Adm ■ www.downeastwindjammer.com

Historic schooners and a lobster sloop make day sails through the islands of Frenchman Bay.

10 Allagash Canoe Trips
MAP Y5 ■ Carrabassett ■ 207 280 1551 ■ Open May–Sep ■ Adm ■ Apply on website ■ www.allagashcanoetrips.com

The Allagash River and Chamberlain Lake offer paddling journeys in the North Woods wilderness and good trout fishing as well.

See map on pp122–3

Lobster Pounds

1 **Five Islands Lobster Co**
MAP P4 ▪ 1447 Five Islands Rd, Georgetown ▪ 207 371 2990 ▪ Closed mid-Oct–early May ▪ $

Lobstermen stream in all day as diners at picnic tables crack lobsters, dip the meat in melted butter, and enjoy the view of a perfect harbor.

2 **The Clam Shack**
MAP N5 ▪ On the Bridge, Kennebunkport ▪ 207 967 3321 ▪ Closed mid-Oct–mid-May ▪ $

The Clam Shack

The namesake fried clams are always good, but the real specialty here is the lobster roll.

3 **The Lobster Pound**
MAP Q3 ▪ 2521 Rte 1, Lincolnville Beach ▪ 207 789 5550 ▪ Closed mid-Oct–mid-May ▪ $

Take a dip, then sit on the deck of this classic seafood restaurant to break down a boiled lobster dinner – or dine inside to escape mendicant gulls.

4 **Barnacle Billy's**
MAP N5 ▪ 70 Perkins Cove Rd, Ogunquit ▪ 207 646 5575 ▪ Closed Nov–mid-Apr ▪ $

The bargain-hunter's choice in a pricey resort, Billy's has a full-service restaurant and a bare-bones seafood shack on scenic Perkins Cove.

5 **Shaw's Fish & Lobster Wharf**
MAP P4 ▪ 129 Rte 32, New Harbor ▪ 207 677 2200 ▪ Closed mid-Oct–mid-May ▪ $

A lobster fan's nirvana, Shaw's has great views of the harbor, a raw bar, and a full liquor license (see p67).

6 **Boothbay Lobster Wharf**
MAP P4 ▪ 97 Atlantic Ave, Boothbay Harbor ▪ 207 633 4900 ▪ Closed mid-Oct–mid-May ▪ $$

In a legendary lobstering harbor, the Lobster Wharf has the shortest possible distance from trap to plate.

7 **Trenton Bridge Lobster Pound**
MAP R3 ▪ 1237 Bar Harbor Rd, Trenton ▪ 207 667 2977 ▪ Closed mid-Oct–late Apr ▪ $

Lobster, nutcrackers, picks, and heaps of paper napkins are really all you need, and this pound barely on the main-land side from Mount Desert Island is a bargain spot for authentic experiences. BYOB.

8 **Bayley's Lobster Pound**
MAP N5 ▪ 9 Ave 6, Pine Point, Scarborough ▪ 207 883 4571 ▪ Closed mid-Oct–late Apr ▪ $

Founded in 1915, there are some great specialties offered here, like lobster-stuffed mushrooms and excellent crabcakes.

9 **Cape Neddick Harborside Restaurant**
MAP N5 ▪ 60 Shore Rd, Cape Neddick ▪ 207 363 5471 ▪ Ring for winter hours ▪ $$

Sample the steamed mussels or clams first, before cracking into the main attraction on the menu.

Cape Neddick Harborside Restaurant

10 **Cook's Lobster & Ale House**
MAP P4 ▪ 68 Garrison Cove Rd, Bailey Island ▪ 207 833 2818 ▪ $

Enjoy your lobster surrounded on three sides by water, with a view of the world's only crib-stone bridge.

Restaurants

PRICE CATEGORIES

For a three course meal for one with half a bottle of wine (or equivalent meal), taxes and extra charges.

$ under $40 $$ $40–$65 $$$ over $65

1 Dockside

MAP N6 ▪ 22 Harris Island Rd, York ▪ 207 363 2868 ▪ Closed Nov–May ▪ $$

An island location in York Harbor makes fish the natural dish, from haddock, cod, and lobster to diver scallops and clams from nearby beds. Bouillabaisse of Maine seafood is always a good bet.

2 Eventide Oyster Co

MAP N4 ▪ 86 Middle St, Portland ▪ 207 774 8538 ▪ Open L, D daily ▪ $$

Favored by hipsters, this eatery serves an array of fresh oysters and other local delicacies of the sea. An extensive wine list and craft beers are on offer here.

3 Primo Restaurant

MAP Q3 ▪ 2 S Main St, Rockland ▪ 207 596 0770 ▪ Closed L, Tue, ring for winter hours ▪ $$$

The chef here conjures up culinary wonders from mostly home-grown produce – even Brussels sprouts get to be stars in season.

4 White Barn Inn

MAP N5 ▪ 37 Beach Ave, Kennebunkport ▪ 207 967 2321 ▪ Closed L ▪ Reservations essential; jacket required for men ▪ $$$

Two 1820s barns make a surprisingly elegant and restful space in which to enjoy the four-course tasting menu.

5 Vignola Cinque Terre

MAP N4 ▪ 10 Dana St, Portland ▪ 207 772 1330 ▪ Open L, D Mon–Fri, D Sat–Sun ▪ $$

Much of the organic produce that goes into the spectacular Ligurian dishes is grown on a nearby farm.

6 Chase's Daily

MAP Q3 ▪ 96 Main St, Belfast ▪ 207 338 0555 ▪ Open Tue–Sat B, L, Sun brunch ▪ $

Back-to-the-land farmers launched this high quality combined bakery, restaurant, and art gallery.

Neons light up Moody's Diner

7 Moody's Diner

MAP Q3 ▪ 1885 Rte 1, Waldoboro ▪ 207 832 7785 ▪ Open B, L, D daily ▪ $

Vacationers and Mainers rub elbows in this iconic diner. Try the blueberry muffins, or the turkey dinner followed by walnut pie.

8 Fore Street

MAP N4 ▪ 288 Fore St, Portland ▪ 207 775 2717 ▪ Closed L ▪ Reservations essential ▪ $$

Sample the wildly popular wood-oven roasted mussels from a menu built largely around local ingredients.

9 Rupununi

MAP R3 ▪ 119 Maine St, Bar Harbor ▪ 207 288 2886 ▪ Closed Nov–Apr ▪ $$

This American bar and grill has steaks and burgers for landlubbers and lobster for seafood fans.

10 Natalie's

MAP Q3 ▪ Camden Harbour Inn, 83 Bay View St, Camden ▪ 207 236 7008 ▪ Closed L ▪ $$$

Penobscot Bay seafood and local produce underpin the elegant contemporary regional cooking, offered in 3-course and 7-course menus.

See map on pp122–3

Artisan Shops

 Tandem Glass
MAP P3 ▪ 6 Eagle Lodge Lane, Dresden

Terrill and Charlie Jenkins have been crafting attractive hand blown art glass since 2006, at their saltbox barn studio and gallery, located northwest of Wiscasset.

Weathervanes of Maine

 Weathervanes of Maine

MAP N5 ▪ 1451 Rte 1, Wells

Weathervanes once topped every Maine barn. This company helps keep the tradition alive, with its menagerie of hand-crafted copper animals, from a jaunty rooster to a flying pig or a dolphin.

3 Thos. Moser Cabinetmakers

MAP P4 ▪ 149 Main St, Freeport

You might pick up some home decorating tips in this restored 19th-century home, where contemporary paintings and photography are displayed next to the cabinetmakers' furniture.

4 Edgecomb Potters Gallery and Studio Complex

MAP P4 ▪ 727 Boothbay Rd, Rte 27S, Edgecomb

Richly colored glazes are the hallmark of Edgecomb porcelain, which is on sale here alongside pieces by other artisans, working in wood, metal, and glass.

5 Maine Artisans

MAP Q3 ▪ 2518 Atlantic Hwy, Lincolnville Beach

Representing the creativity of midcoast Maine, this cooperative gallery of local artisans sells colorful knitted socks and driftwood lamps, delicate glass orchids, and paintings on slate, among other wares.

6 Swans Island Blankets

MAP Q3 ▪ 231 Rte 1, Northport

An elegant pure-wool Swans Island blanket is the ultimate word in cold-weather luxury. The Northport showroom-studio is set in a lovely converted 1780s farmhouse.

7 Bluejacket Ship Crafters

MAP Q3 ▪ 160 E Main St, Searsport

The oldest ship-modeling company in the country has more than 100 historically accurate examples on display. Select a kit for a sailing sloop, or radio-controlled lobster boat.

8 Rackliffe Pottery

MAP R3 ▪ 130 Ellsworth Rd, Blue Hill

Stop off at this workshop overlooking Blue Hill Bay and you might see artisans throwing dishware on a potter's wheel. A blueberry bowl makes a perfect souvenir of Maine.

9 Abbe Museum

MAP R3 ▪ 26 Mount Desert St, Rte 3, Bar Harbor

The gift shop of this small museum has highly prized sweetgrass, ash, and birchbark baskets made by Maine's Native peoples.

10 Columbia Falls Pottery

MAP R2 ▪ 150 Main St, Columbia Falls

It seems as if the artists at this pottery simply look out the window for inspiration for their tiles, clocks, lamps, and crocks, all decorated with painted blueberries, lupines, sailboats, and shore birds.

Antiques Shops

 1 York Antiques Gallery
MAP N5 ■ 746 Rte 1, York

Dealers at this gallery specialize in fine 18th- and 19th-century furniture and accessories. You probably won't find a bargain, but you might pick up decorating ideas.

2 Hutchins' Antiques Etc
MAP N5 ■ 166 Main St, Ogunquit

After a lazy morning on Ogunquit beach, peruse the offerings in this nearby family-owned shop. Dealers lean toward small objects of desire – jewelry, glass, porcelain, linens, and nifty little kitchen items.

3 Douglas N. Harding Rare Books
MAP N5 ■ 2152 Post Rd, Rte 1, Wells

You'll find volumes on everything from circus arts to UFOs in this 14-room shop with more than 100,000 used and rare books.

4 Smith-Zukas Antiques
MAP N5 ■ 1755 Post Rd, Rte 1, Wells

Each of the buildings in this inviting complex has a distinctive personality, with an eclectic mix of offerings from formal furnishings to shabby-chic accessories, and architectural ornaments to garden statuary.

items for sale at Smith-Zukas Antiques

5 Victorian Lighting
MAP N5 ■ 29 York St, Rte 1, Kennebunk

Despite the name, this illuminating shop carries high-quality lighting fixtures from the 1840s right through to the 1930s, restored and rewired for modern homes. Select a simple sconce or a showpiece chandelier.

6 Marston House Antiques
MAP P4 ■ 101 Main St, Wiscasset

The proprietors also own a home in a French village, so the shop's furniture, soft linens, clay pots, wire garden stands, and stoneware serving pieces all have Gallic flair.

7 Pumpkin Patch Antiques
MAP Q3 ■ 15 Rte 1, Searsport

Country furniture and a lovely selection of mid-20th-century quilts highlight the domestic antiques in this small shop. Nautical items and Chinese porcelain are reminders of Searsport's maritime heyday.

8 Cabot Mill Antiques
MAP P4 ■ 14 Main St, Brunswick

This restored brick textile mill has 160 booths that feature folk art, nautical antiques, furniture, art, pottery, and jewelry.

9 Antiques USA
MAP N5 ■ Rte 1, Arundel

Route 1 from York to Arundel is dense with antiques shops. Antiques USA is one of the largest, bringing hundreds of dealers with different tastes and interests under one roof.

10 Big Chicken Barn Books & Antiques
MAP R3 ■ 1768 Bucksport Rd, Ellsworth

The proprietors of this gigantic emporium encourage browsers to bring a picnic lunch. It takes hours to peruse the thousands of magazines, rare books, and antiques.

See map on pp122–3

Streetsmart

**Oak Bluffs' gingerbread cottages,
Martha's Vineyard, Massachusetts**

Getting To and Around New England

Arriving by Air

Logan International Airport in Boston is the principal gateway airport to New England. Located only 3 miles (5 km) from downtown Boston, Logan is an efficient airport with ample parking. Terminal E handles international arrivals but international departures may take off from other terminals.

The cheapest and quickest method to make your way into the city from Logan International Airport is via the free **MBTA** Silver Line buses that run to South Station.

A few international flights also arrive at Connecticut's **Bradley International Airport**. **T.F. Green Airport** in Providence, Rhode Island, and **Manchester Boston Regional Airport** in New Hampshire are used by a few European budget carriers and they often provide the most inexpensive domestic air fares to New England. **Portland Jetport** is a good gateway for domestic airlines.

Arriving by Rail

Amtrak trains serve coastal and central New England as far north as Brunswick, Maine. Travelers from overseas can buy passes for discounted Amtrak travel throughout the US.

Arriving by Bus

Peter Pan has stops in western Massachusetts and Connecticut; **Concord Coach Lines** serves New Hampshire and Maine; **Plymouth & Brockton** covers southeastern Massachusetts; national carrier **Greyhound** and its subsidiaries cover almost everywhere.

Arriving by Car

From the west, I-90 enters Massachusetts from New York State and ends at Logan Airport. From the south, I-95 follows the coast up to Boston, then heads north through New Hampshire to Maine. From the northwest, I-89 and I-91 enter Vermont from Quebec. I-89 cuts southeast to Boston; I-91 goes south to New York via Connecticut and Massachusetts.

Traveling by Train

Amtrak runs a fast train service between New York and Boston, with connections running to Hartford, Brunswick, Providence, Springfield, St. Albans, and Burlington.

Traveling by Bus

Most cities have a local bus service. Intercity bus transportation can be arranged on the Concord, Plymouth & Brockton, Peter Pan, and Greyhound lines.

Traveling by Ferry

Ferries are essential for visiting islands, but Boston is also served by commuter ferries from the North and South shores. They are operated by **Boston Harbor Cruises** or the MBTA.

Traveling by Car

In Boston, driving should be left to taxi drivers. In the rest of New England, however, it is usually the best way to get around, see the countryside, stop when you want to, and explore the byways and rural back roads.

To drive in New England you will need a current driver's license from your home state or country. Most car rental agencies also ask to see the passports of foreign nationals. Airports usually have the most complete range of rental agencies, including **Avis**, **Enterprise**, **Budget**, **National**, and **Hertz**.

To rent a car, drivers must be between the ages of 25 and 75. Apart from your driver's license, you will need a major credit card as a deposit (very few rental agencies accept cash). Even if your personal insurance covers you, you should generally accept the Collision (or Loss) Damage Waiver to avoid financial entanglements in case of an accident.

Traveling by Metro

Boston is the only New England city with a subway and light-rail system. The "T" (as it is called locally) has a stop within a few blocks of almost every central city sight, and extends into the suburbs, often as above-ground light rail.

MBTA sells Charlie Cards at many subway stations. The smart card, which can be loaded with money or a T-Pass, discounts each ride by about 15 percent and also works for harbor ferries and buses. MBTA's LinkPass offers one or seven days' discounted travel on the metro, bus, inner-harbor ferry, and the inner ring of commuter rail.

Traveling by Plane

New England is too small to sustain many regional carriers, but **Cape Air** frequently flies small planes between Boston, Nantucket, and Martha's Vineyard. In summer, Cape Air also flies to Boston from Vermont, Maine, and New Hampshire.

Cycling

Cycling is a great way to explore the New England countryside. Dedicated trails along former railroad rights-of-way are found throughout the region. The national **Rails to Trails Conservancy** maintains a useful website. When sharing the roads, try to stay on the right-hand shoulder to avoid being hit. By law, children under 12 must use helmets.

Walking

Many towns maintain scenic walking paths, some linking communities along trails that can stretch as far as 30 miles (48 km). To explore what is available in the area you're visiting, go to the **American Trails** website for regional links within the state trails section.

Hiking is a satisfying way to explore the New England states; the main long-distance route traversing the region is the Appalachian Trail.

DIRECTORY

ARRIVING BY AIR

Bradley International Airport (BDL)
MAP C4 ■ Windsor Locks, CT
📞 860 292 2000
🌐 bradleyairport.com

Logan International Airport (BOS)
MAP F2 ■ Boston, MA
📞 800 235 6426
🌐 massport.com

Manchester-Boston Regional Airport (MHT)
MAP M6 ■ Manchester, NH
📞 603 624 6556
🌐 flymanchester.com

MBTA
📞 617 222 5000
🌐 mbta.com

Portland Jetport (PWM)
MAP N4 ■ Portland, ME
📞 207 774 7301
🌐 portlandjetport.org

T.F. Green Airport (PVD)
MAP E4 ■ Warwick, (Providence), RI
📞 401 737 8222
🌐 pvdairport.com

ARRIVING BY RAIL

Amtrak
📞 800 872 7245
🌐 amtrak.com

ARRIVING BY BUS

Concord Coach Lines
📞 800 639 3317
🌐 concordcoachlines.com

Greyhound
📞 800 231 2222
🌐 greyhound.com

Peter Pan
📞 800 343 9999
🌐 peterpanbus.com

Plymouth & Brockton
📞 508 746 0378
🌐 p-b.com

TRAVELING BY FERRY

Boston Harbor Cruises
📞 617 227 4321
🌐 bostonharborcruises.com

TRAVELING BY CAR

Avis
📞 800 331 1212
🌐 avis.com

Budget
📞 800 527 7000
🌐 budget.com

Enterprise
📞 800 736 8222
🌐 enterprise.com

Hertz
📞 800 654 3131
🌐 hertz.com

National
📞 800 227 7368
🌐 nationalcar.com

TRAVELING BY PLANE

Cape Air
📞 800 227 3247, 508 771 6944 (from outside the US)
🌐 flycapeair.com

CYCLING

Rails to Trails Conservancy
🌐 traillink.com

WALKING

American Trails
P.O. Box 491797 Redding, CA 96049-1797
📞 530 605 4395
🌐 americantrails.org

Practical Information

Passports and Visas

Everyone entering the US must have a machine-readable biometric passport. Citizens of the EU and other visa-waiver countries must apply for entry at least 72 hours ahead of travel by filing an online ESTA form at the **US Customs and Border Protection**.

Consulates within the US, including those of the **UK**, **Australia**, **New Zealand**, and **Canada**, are unable to intervene in legal matters, but can provide limited services for visiting nationals.

Customs Regulations

Visitors over 21 may bring two pints (1 l) of alcohol; 200 cigarettes, 50 cigars, or 4 lb (2 kg) of smoking tobacco; and gifts worth up to $100. Meats, fresh cheeses, live plants, and produce are prohibited. Travelers bringing in $10,000 or more in cash must declare the money at customs.

Travel Safety Advice

Visitors can get up-to-date travel safety information from the **US Department of State**, from the **Australian Department of Foreign Affairs and Trade**, and from the **UK Foreign and Commonwealth Office**. For further information, check the **US Department of Homeland Security**'s online National Terrorism Advisory System. Security is a high priority at New England airports; be prepared for long lines at passport control. Make sure all your baggage, including carry-on, is clearly marked with ID. Pack carry-on liquids in a clear plastic bag.

Travel Insurance

Buy comprehensive travel insurance before your trip. Emergency medical or dental treatment is expensive, and proof of insurance is all but mandatory. A good policy will also pay to replace lost or stolen property. You may need extra cover for certain activities, such as skiing.

Health

No vaccinations are necessary to visit New England. Always bring along extra medications as well as copies of any prescriptions. Your hotel can refer you to the nearest pharmacy or to a hospital if you need emergency care. To avoid catching Lyme disease from ticks, use insect repellent and keep arms, legs, and ankles covered when walking through woods and fields.

Personal Security

Know the escape route from your hotel room in case of fire. Secure your door with a chain and use the peephole to confirm the identity of anyone who knocks. Keep valuables in the room or hotel safe, along with a separate copy of your credit card numbers and their help-line numbers in case of loss or theft. Despite the sensationalism of TV dramas in the US, the occurrence of muggings, thefts, murder and other mayhem is low in the country, and lower than average in New England.

Nevertheless, don't court trouble. Avoid poorly lit and deserted areas late at night. Know where you are going, and walk purposefully. Carry only small amounts of cash and if confronted by a mugger, give up your money promptly.

Emergency Services

If you need to phone the emergency hotline number for **fire**, **police**, or an **ambulance**, stay on the line even if you are unable to speak in order to allow the emergency locator system to track you. All emergency calls are free.

Disabled Travelers

Wheelchair-accessible entrances and restrooms are mandatory for public facilities built since 1987, except historic buildings and most B&Bs. For more information on accessibility, contact **SATH**, the Society for Accessible Travel and Hospitality.

Trips and Tours

Several different walking tours are available in Boston, most departing from the Information Center located on Boston Common. Many free walking tours, including the Freedom Trail, are offered by the rangers of the **Boston National Historical Park**. **Old Town Trolley Tours** and **Beantown Trolley Tours** offer hop-on-hop-off sightseeing buses with narrated rides around the city. They can be picked up anywhere along their routes. With **Boston Duck Tours** visitors board an amphibious vehicle for a city tour combined with a plunge into the Charles River. Trips leave from the Museum of Science and Prudential Tower.

A diverse selection of active trips and tours cover other parts of New England. There are several companies that can arrange two- to five-day hiking excursions in the beautiful New England countryside. One of the best and most established operators is **New England Hiking Holidays**.

Likewise, several outfitters organize multi-day group bicycling tours in some of the most scenic parts of Vermont and Maine. One of the most popular is **VBT**.

The Allagash Waterway undoubtedly provides the ultimate canoeing adventure in New England, while various outfitters will arrange white-water river rafting trips *(see p56)* in Maine. Many expert sea kayakers tackle the popular Maine Island Trail from Portland to Machias on their own. Contact the **Maine Island Trail** **Association** for details. Sailing vacations, largely aboard schooner-rigged vessels called wind-jammers, are popular on the Maine coast. Most of these encourage travelers to help rig and haul sails. To participate in such an excursion contact the **Maine Windjammer Association** or **Maine Windjammer Cruises**.

Backwoods Maine has a long tradition of "sporting camps," which are usually based in remote locations and are often accessible only by float plane. Here, campers can commune with nature by paddling, fishing, and hiking. For more information see the **Maine Sporting Camp Association** website.

DIRECTORY

PASSPORTS AND VISAS

Australian Consulate
150 E 42d St, 34th Fl,
New York, NY 10017
212 351 6500
newyork.consulate.
gov.au

Canadian Consulate
3 Copley Pl, Suite 400,
Boston, MA 02116
617 247 5100
can-am.gc.ca/boston

New Zealand Consulate
222 E. 41st St,
Suite 2510,
New York, NY 10017
212 832 4038
nzembassy.com/
united-states-of-america

UK Consulate
1 Broadway,
Boston, MA 02210
617 245 4500
ukinusa.fco.gov.uk

US Customs and Border Protection
esta.cbp.dhs.gov/esta

TRAVEL SAFETY ADVICE

Australian Department of Foreign Affairs and Trade
dfat.gov.au
smartraveller.gov.au

UK Foreign and Commonwealth Office
gov.uk/foreign-travel-advice

US Department of Homeland Security
dhs.gov/national-terrorism-advisory-system

US Department of State
travel.state.gov

EMERGENCY SERVICES

Fire, Police, Ambulance
911

DISABLED TRAVELERS

SATH
sath.org

TRIPS AND TOURS

Beantown Trolley Tours
brushhilltours.com

Boston Duck Tours
bostonducktours.com

Boston National Historical Park
nps.gov/bost

Maine Island Trail Association
mita.org

Maine Sporting Camp Association
mainesportingcamps.com

Maine Windjammer Association
sailmainecoast.com

Maine Windjammer Cruises
mainewindjammercruises.com

New England Hiking Holidays
nehikingholidays.com

Old Town Trolley Tours
trolleytours.com/boston

VBT
vbt.com

Currency and Banking

Money in the United States of America comes in dollars, which are divided into 100 cents. Coins come in denominations of 1, 5, 10, 25, and 50 cents, and 1 dollar. Dollar coins are used mostly to buy from vending machines, while 50-cent pieces are rare. The quarter (the 25-cent piece) is the handiest coin for vending machines and parking meters.

Notes (bills) come in denominations of $1, $5, $10, $20, $50, and $100. Small businesses will often decline $50 and $100 bills.

Currency exchange facilities are available at the main branches of the larger banks, but harder to find elsewhere. In general, you will get a better rate making ATM withdrawals than by exchanging cash, even taking into account the additional banking fees.

ATMs are usually found near the entrances of the bank branch. The main banking systems that are honored in the US are Cirrus, Plus, and NYCE. Most ATMs also accept MasterCard and Visa credit cards. Many shops will let you pay with a debit card and get cash back – usually fee free.

Dollar-denominated traveler's checks issued by American Express or Thomas Cook are widely accepted, but personal checks drawn on foreign banks – or even out-of-state banks – are not.

Using a credit card is generally much safer than carrying cash, and essential for renting a car or reserving a hotel room. MasterCard and Visa credit cards are almost universally accepted, as is the Discover card. American Express is also widely accepted, but small merchants tend to balk at the company's high fees. Diners Club is accepted at some high-end establishments.

Internet

Many hotels, B&Bs, and motels provide Wi-Fi Internet access for travelers carrying their own devices. Free and open Wi-Fi is also usually found at public libraries, coffee shops, as well as many public parks.

Telephone

Pay phones are rare, and when you do manage to find one, it will usually accept coins, charging 50 cents to $1 for a local call. The cheapest way to call is by using a prepaid calling card available at gas stations, convenience stores, and newsstands.

Note that calls within greater Boston require dialing the area code in addition to the 7-digit phone number. Dial 1 for long-distance calls within the US and Canada, or 011 for calls to other countries.

If you have an unlocked cell phone that operates on the GSM bands, you can also purchase a SIM card for AT&T or T-Mobile service on a pay-as-you-go basis. Many Target, WalMart, and Radio Shack stores sell disposable phones for as little as $15; calling minutes cost extra.

US Postal Services

The majority of post offices are open from 8am to 6pm Monday to Friday and 8am to noon Saturday. Properly stamped letters and packages less than 12 oz (340 g) can be dropped into blue mailboxes. For current rates, see the **US Postal Service** website.

Newspapers and Magazines

Although the dominant newspaper in the region is the *Boston Globe*, the *New York Times*, the *Wall Street Journal*, and *USA Today* are also popular. For entertainment listings outside Boston, check local papers. *Yankee Magazine* has an online guide and the website of the *Boston Globe* is also a valuable source of local information and listings.

Television and Radio

Most lodgings with television provide "basic" cable that includes local stations, broadcast networks, and a handful of cable-only channels. Local radio is found on the FM band (88–108mHz).

Opening Hours

Most attractions and stores open daily, but many museums close on Mondays. Museums are typically open from 10am to 6pm on weekdays, from 10am to 5pm on Saturday, and from noon to 5pm on Sunday. Hours and days of opening may be reduced in winter so it is best to check beforehand with the venues. Shops typically open from 9 or 10am and close at 6pm in business districts and at 9 or 10pm in shopping centers (they close at 6pm on the weekend).

Some banks open on Saturday morning, but outside of the bigger cities many are closed on the weekend.

Time Difference

New England is in the Eastern time zone: GMT minus five hours.

Daylight saving time (EDT) begins at 2am on the second Sunday in March and reverts to standard time (EST) at 2am on the first Sunday in November. During EDT, the local time is GMT minus four hours.

Electrical Appliances

Electrical appliances in the United States operate on 110–120 volts, 60 cycles, and use a polar- ized two-prong plug with flat blades. In order to use non-US single-voltage appliances you will need an adapter and voltage converter, both of which are quite commonly available at airport shops and some department and electrical stores. The majority of laptops and travel appliances are dual- voltage, and many hotels have dual-voltage sockets for electric shavers. US phone systems use an RJ11 connector.

Weather

New England weather can vary quite widely. Daytime temperatures from December through February are usually freezing or even colder, while July and August daytime highs can often exceed 80°F (27°C), accompanied by high humidity. September and October are usually cool and dry, while November and March are chilly and damp. Spring weather ranges from warm sun to windy rain. Northerly areas are generally 10°F (7°C) cooler.

Given the changeable weather, it makes sense to dress in layers, with a sweater or jacket for cool summer evenings. Be sure to pack a folding umbrella, sunglasses, and comfortable walking shoes. In midwinter, a warm coat, scarf, gloves, and a hat that protects your ears are necessities, and boots are advised.

While New England is a year-round destination, tourism is busiest from late June through mid- October, and from around Christmas through to late February in ski country.

Cheaper accommodation can often be found from late April into late May, and late October, but some rural attractions may only be open on weekends at these times of the year.

Visitor Information

Discover New England focuses on the tourism resources of the six New England states. The **Maine Office of Tourism**, **Massachusetts Office of Travel and Tourism**, **Vermont Department of Tourism**, **New Hampshire Travel and Tourism**, **Rhode Island Tourism**, and **Connecticut Office of Tourism** each have useful online tourism guides to the region, with a range of helpful resources. The **Greater Boston CVB** (Convention and Visitors Bureau) website also offers useful advice.

DIRECTORY

US POSTAL SERVICES

US Postal Service
w usps.com

NEWSPAPERS AND MAGAZINES

Boston Globe
w bostonglobe.com

New York Times
w nytimes.com

USA Today
w usatoday.com

Wall Street Journal
w wsj.com

Yankee Magazine
w newengland.com

VISITOR INFORMATION

Connecticut Office of Tourism
w ctvisit.com

Discover New England
w discovernewengland.org

Greater Boston CVB
w bostonusa.com

Maine Office of Tourism
w visitmaine.com

Massachusetts Office of Travel and Tourism
w massvacation.com

New Hampshire Travel and Tourism
w visitnh.com

Rhode Island Tourism
w visitrhodeisland.com

Vermont Department of Tourism
w vermontvacation.com

Shopping

Visitors from overseas consider clothes shopping in New England a highlight of their visit since lower taxes reduce the cost of apparel. Although most states levy a sales tax of 6.2 to 7.5 percent, New Hampshire has none. Massachusetts does not levy tax on clothing and footwear items that cost less than $175.

Household linens are often discounted at the January "white sales," winter apparel in March and April, and summer apparel in September. Best prices on brand-name items are usually found at the factory outlet stores. These cluster in malls, especially in North Conway, New Hampshire; Freeport and Kittery, Maine; Manchester, Vermont; and Wrentham, Massachusetts.

Where to Eat

Travelers can eat well in New England without breaking the bank. Even casual luncheonettes and diners will often feature local seafood, meats, and fruits and vegetables. The dominant "cuisine" here is American, a melting pot of flavors from around the world. Hamburgers in the US are unrivaled. The top ethnic cuisine is Italian (or Italian-American, which is heavier on pasta and red sauce), while Mexican, Thai, and pizza dominate the budget category.

Places to eat come in many shapes and sizes. Any place that calls itself a diner, whether it is a roadside dining car or just a small storefront, will typically feature casual, home-style cooking. Those looking for quick bites on the go, especially in cities, should focus on food trucks, most of which serve only a few specialized items (two popular Boston trucks often found together specialize in lobster rolls and grilled cheese sand-wiches, respectively).

Restaurants range from very casual places with family-style seating at large tables to temples of haute cuisine that require reservations months in advance or a name that might be found on the front page of a tabloid.

Most New England bars also serve food, and a more casual and less expensive restaurant bar menu might be just what you're looking for – no reservations required. The legal minimum drinking age in New England is 21, and photo ID may be needed to enter a bar.

Children are welcome almost everywhere and many restaurants in tourist areas feature children's menus.

Along the coast, look for places that serve seafood in the rough. Ultra-casual and usually located by the ocean, these spots focus on steamed lobster and clams and fried seafood. They generally feature a counter to place orders, and picnic tables for eating al fresco. In Maine, The Lobster Pound (see p128) is a culinary icon for its particular style of seafood in the rough.

American restaurants generally pay waitstaff only a token wage and count on diners to make up the difference with tips. For good service, tip 20 percent. For counter or window service, loose change or a dollar should go into the tip bucket.

Where to Stay

New England's highly varied accommodations can suit almost all tastes and budgets. During the summer vacation season and during fall foliage, lodgings can sometimes be hard to come by, so it is always best to book in advance. Many lodgings require a minimum stay of two or three nights during holiday periods, summer high season, or weekends during foliage season – unless rooms are still available at the last minute.

State and local lodging and sales taxes can add as much as 19 percent to your bill and the charges are inescapable. Resorts often charge 15 to 20 percent either for staff gratuities or as a "resort fee" for facilities.

Hotel and motel chains are not known for their individuality; they thrive on providing their guests a consistent, predictable product. But they often offer discounts for mul-tiple bookings, as well as free nights through their loyalty programs. All the major global and national chains and hotel groups are represented across New England, but as the lodgings included in this guide prize local charac-ter, few of the listings belong to these groups.

Motels usually offer the best combination of price and convenience for travelers who do their own driving. A standard motel room has a color TV, heat and air conditioning, and private bathroom. More modern places usually have two double beds, making it easier to fit the whole family in a single room. Some chains permit under-12s to stay free.

Most American lodgings that identify as B&Bs are variants on the country inn, with private en-suite rooms and a hot cooked breakfast at a communal table. Country inns, on the other hand, are usually more like small boutique hotels in the countryside. Some have attached restaurants and may have swimming pools or gardens. The websites of the **New England Inns and Resorts Association**, **Bed and Breakfast Associates Bay Colony**, and **Bed & Breakfast Agency of Boston** have useful B&B and inn listings.

New England's hostel network is sparse but some hostels can be found at prime locations, including Boston and Cape Cod. A list of member hostels and their locations is available from **Hostelling International/ American Youth Hostels** (HI/AYH). The **HI/AYH Eastern New England Council** provides information on hostels in New Hampshire, Maine, and Massachusetts. **Boston International Youth Hostel** is also a good hotel resource.

AirBnB has drastically enlarged room inventories throughout New England with offerings that range from a room in an apartment to entire apartments or houses. Read postings carefully, as some locations can be inconvenient or in marginal neighborhoods. AirBnB is for travelers who do not expect much

hand-holding. Many of the properties have their own cooking and laundry facilities, which can save both time and money.

Government-operated campgrounds in state and national parks and forests tend to operate late May to mid-October, while private campgrounds may extend the season in both directions if the weather cooperates. Sites will vary from primitive (with running water and toilets) to rather posh, with hot showers, facilities for cooking, and electric and sanitary hookups for motor homes. The **Maine**, **New Hampshire** and **Connecticut Campground Owners Associations** are useful resources. Also make sure to check the camping sections on conservation department and national and state park websites.

DIRECTORY

WHERE TO STAY

AirBnB
ⓦ airbnb.com

Bed & Breakfast Agency of Boston
Ⓒ 800 248 9262 or 617 720 3540; 0800 895128 from the UK
ⓦ boston-bnbagency.com

Bed and Breakfast Associates Bay Colony
PO Box 57166, Babson Park Branch, Boston, MA
Ⓒ 888 486 6018 or 617 720 0522
ⓦ bnbboston.com

Boston International Youth Hostel
12 Hemenway St, Boston, MA 02115
Ⓒ 617 536 9455
ⓦ bostonhostel.org

Connecticut Campground Owners Association
1728 Route 198, Woodstock, CT 06281
Ⓒ 860 521 4704
ⓦ campconn.com

Hostelling International/American Youth Hostels
8401 Colesville Rd, Suite 600, Silver Spring, MD 20910
Ⓒ 301 495 1240 or 800 909 4776
ⓦ hiusa.org

HI/AYH Eastern New England Council
218 Holland St, Somerville, MA 02144
Ⓒ 617 718 7990
ⓦ hinewengland.org

Maine Campground Owners Association
10 Falcon Rd, Suite 1, Lewiston, ME 04240
Ⓒ 207 782 5874
ⓦ campmaine.com

New England Inns and Resorts Association
PO Box 1089, 44 Lafayette Road, North Hampton, NH 03862
Ⓒ 603 964 6689
ⓦ newengland innsandresorts.com

New Hampshire Campground Owners Association
PO Box 1074, Epsom, NH 03234
Ⓒ 800 822 6764
ⓦ ucampnh.com

Places to Stay

Boston Lodgings with Character

Beacon Hill Hotel & Bistro
MAP V4 ■ 25 Charles St, Boston, MA 02114 ■ 617 723 7575 ■ www.beacon hillhotel.com ■ $$
This smart boutique hotel near Boston Common has the feel of a family-run Parisian hotel. Rooms may be small but are very chic; a sitting room and private roof deck offer space to spread out. Breakfast is included.

Charles Hotel
MAP F2 ■ 1 Bennett St, Cambridge, MA 02138 ■ 617 864 1200 ■ www.charleshotel.com ■ $$
Visiting celebrities and academics love the Charles's hallmark style – a spare modernism softened by such homey touches as custom quilts on the beds. The hotel's attractive plaza hosts a lively farmers' market and outdoor dining during the summer months.

Charlesmark Hotel
MAP U5 ■ 655 Boylston St, Boston, MA 02116 ■ 617 247 1212 ■ www.charles markhotel.com ■ $$
In an 1892 townhouse, the Charlesmark resembles contemporary European urban boutique hotels, with its tiny lobby, compact rooms, and high-concept design. Breakfast is included.

Fairmont Copley Plaza Hotel
MAP U5 ■ 138 St James Ave, Boston, MA 02116 ■ 617 267 5300 ■ www.fairmont.com/copley-plaza-boston ■ $$
All 383 rooms in this Edwardian grande dame on Copley Square in the heart of Back Bay have been renovated, updating the traditional genteel style of dark woods and rich fabrics.

The Godfrey Hotel Boston
MAP W4 ■ 505 Washington St, Boston, MA 02111 ■ 617 804 2000 ■ www.godfreyhotel boston.com ■ $$
The cornerstone of Downtown Crossing's revitalization, this boutique gem beautifully combines cutting-edge technology with old-fashioned comfort. It's conveniently close to the Financial District for work or the Theater District for play. Very fast Wi-Fi included.

Harborside Inn
MAP X3 ■ 185 State St, Boston, MA 02109 ■ 617 723 7500 ■ www.harbor sideinnboston.com ■ $$
Housed in a granite former spice warehouse, this boutique hotel is located just steps from the harbor and the Faneuil Hall Marketplace. A Boston travel guide is kept in each room.

The Hotel Veritas
MAP F2 ■ 1 Remington St, Cambridge, MA 02138 ■ 617 520 5000 ■ www.thehotelveritas.com ■ $$$
This very buttoned-down and soothing 31-room boutique hotel is a short block from Harvard Yard but just far enough from Harvard Square to avoid the bustle and noise. Amenities (including Wi-Fi) are luxe, personal service is tops, but many guest rooms are small.

Liberty Hotel
MAP V3 ■ 215 Charles St, Boston, MA 02114 ■ 617 224 4000 ■ www.liberty hotel.com ■ $$$
Located at the foot of Beacon Hill, this swanky hotel incorporates the historic granite archi-tecture of the Charles Street Jail with the latest in modern design.

Revere Hotel Boston Common
MAP V4 ■ 200 Stuart St, Boston, MA 02116 ■ 617 482 1800 ■ www.revere hotel.com ■ $$$
Two blocks from Boston Common at the edge of the Theater District, this contemporary luxury hotel has 356 large rooms decorated in minimalist style. The location is convenient for sight-seeing, but can be noisy at night. Wi-Fi is free.

The Verb Hotel
MAP S5 ■ 1271 Boylston St, Boston, MA 02115 ■ 617 566 4500 ■ www.theverbhotel.com ■ $$$
Located behind iconic Fenway Park, The Verb

transformed a generic mid-20th-century motel into Boston's rock and roll hotel. With a pitch-perfect millennial vibe, it's a drumstick's throw from Berklee College of Music. Wi-Fi is free.

In-Town Hotels

The Dean Hotel

MAP E4 ▪ 122 Fountain St, Providence, RI 02903 ▪ 401 455 3326 ▪ www. thedeanhotel.com ▪ $
Contemporary designer chic with a smirk, the Dean even has red lights in the halls to allude to the 1912 building's bordello history. Now it is the millennials' ideal Downcity business hotel with 52 rooms, a beer hall, coffee and karaoke bars, and free Wi-Fi.

Hotel on North

MAP B2 ▪ 297 North St, Pittsfield, MA 01201 ▪ 413 358 4741 ▪ www. hotelonnorth.com ▪ $
The 45 rooms of this boutique hotel in two historic downtown buildings are filled with quirky decor, including furniture made by local artisans. Tech features are cutting-edge, and include very fast, free Wi-Fi. The hotel is great for exploring both the northern and southern Berkshires. The service is attentive without being obsequious.

Hawthorne Hotel

MAP F2 ▪ 18 Washington Sq, Salem, MA 01970 ▪ 978 744 4080 ▪ www. hawthornehotel.com ▪ $$
Constructed in 1925 in the Federal style of a century earlier, the Hawthorne sits near Salem Common

and the Peabody Essex Museum (see p41). The decor is styled on traditional American verging on Colonial. Free Wi-Fi.

Hotel Portsmouth

MAP N6 ▪ 40 Court St, Portsmouth, NH 03801 ▪ 603 433 1200 ▪ www. thehotelportsmouth.com ▪ $$
Soft contemporary styling in 32 rooms complements the historic Queen Anne brick mansion, which is located just off Market Square. In-room iPads, free Wi-Fi, and iPhone docks in each room keep guests connected. The rate includes parking and light breakfast.

Hotel Providence

MAP E4 ▪ 139 Matthewson St, Providence, RI 02903 ▪ 401 861 8000 ▪ www. hotelprovidence.com ▪ $$
Although Providence has a wealth of boutique hotels, this luxurious yet unpretentious downtown place does an excellent job of mixing traditional formality with contemporary design.

Providence Biltmore

MAP E4 ▪ 11 Dorrance St, Providence, RI 02903 ▪ 401 421 0700 ▪ www. providencebiltmore.com ▪ $$
This 1922 downtown mini-skyscraper was completely renovated to create smartly appointed rooms in contemporary style with comfortable beds, heavy draperies, and deluxe linens. The regular rooms tend to be small, making junior suites a better bet for longer stays.

Sheraton Portsmouth Harborside Hotel

MAP N6 ▪ 250 Market St, Portsmouth, NH 03801 ▪ 603 431 2300 ▪ www. sheratonportsmouth.com ▪ $$
Standing two blocks from Market Square and next to the whale-watch and harbor cruise docks, this modern business hotel is equally well suited to the leisure traveler. A redwood sauna, large pool, and an extensive fitness room set it apart from other Portsmouth lodgings.

Six South Street Hotel

MAP L4 ▪ 6 E South St, Hanover, NH 03755 ▪ 603 643 0600 ▪ www. sixsouth.com ▪ $$
Although marketed to families visiting students at Dartmouth, this contemporary boutique hotel is a good base for touring New Hampshire and Vermont from the upper Connecticut River Valley. There is a lively lounge and restaurant on site. Very fast Wi-Fi included.

The Study at Yale

MAP C5 ▪ 1157 Chapel St, New Haven, CT 06511 ▪ 203 503 3900 ▪ www. studyatyale.com ▪ $$
Facing the Yale School of Art in the midst of Yale's most striking modern architecture, The Study is almost self-consciously sleek and up-to-date, with flat-screen TV, free Wi-Fi access, and iPod docking station on the clock radio. The main floor includes three walnut-paneled meeting rooms, a bar, and the inspired Heirloom restaurant.

The Attwater

MAP F5 ▪ 22 Liberty St, Newport, RI 02840 ▪ 401 846 7444 ▪ www.the attwater.com ▪ $$$

Located in a residential neighborhood just three blocks away from the waterfront, this 17-room boutique hotel is a breath of fresh air in often stuffy Newport. All of the fresh rooms are bright and colorful and feature fridges, iPads, free Wi-Fi, and beach bags for a walk to the sands. The room rate includes light breakfast.

Hotel Vermont

MAP J3 ▪ 41 Cherry St, Burlington, VT 05401 ▪ 802 651 0080 ▪ hotelvt. com ▪ $$$

This stylish downtown hotel features Vermont-made blankets, local craftsmanship, and contemporary artwork. Super-fast Wi-Fi is part of the hotel package, along with multiple ports for recharging mobile gear. DIY laundry facilities are a boon for light travelers. Free bicycles and paid yoga classes available.

Press Hotel, Autograph Collection

MAP N4 ▪ 119 Exchange St, Portland, ME 04101 ▪ 207 808 8800 ▪ www. thepresshotel.com ▪ $$$

This newspaper building from the mid-1920s was transformed in 2015 into an upscale Old Port luxury hotel. The 110 spacious guest rooms have oversized windows, vintage-style writing desks, marble baths, and playful newsroom references. USB and power ports abound, and Wi-Fi is free.

Country Inns (Southern)

The Inn at Woodstock Hill

MAP D4 ▪ 94 Plaine Hill Rd, Woodstock, CT 06281 ▪ 860 928 0528 ▪ www. woodstockhill.net ▪ $

The steeply pitched hip roof, multiple dormers, and white clapboard siding make this 1816 inn a visual emblem of rural New England. All rooms have private baths.

Captain Freeman Inn

MAP H4 ▪ 15 Breakwater Rd, Brewster, MA 02631 ▪ 508 896 7481 ▪ www.cap tainfreemaninn.com ▪ $$

The 11 rooms in this 1860s sea captain's home turned B&B are decorated in traditional style but with modern amenities such as free Wi-Fi. The full gourmet breakfast is superb, and the location on the King's Highway is removed from traffic but still close to all that Cape Cod has to offer.

Deerfield Inn

MAP C2 ▪ 81 Main St, Deerfield, MA 01342 ▪ 413 774 5587 ▪ www. deerfieldinn.com ▪ $$

Built in 1884, this country inn sits in the heart of 350-year-old Deerfield. The 24 rooms are all different shapes and sizes, but are consistently decorated in American Colonial Revival style. Historic Deerfield's museum store is on site.

Fife 'n Drum

MAP B4 ▪ 53 N Main St, Kent, CT 06757 ▪ 860 927 3509 ▪ www.fifendrum. com ▪ $$

Eight rooms with vaulted ceilings occupy the main inn next to the Fife 'n Drum

restaurant and there are three more in an adjacent Victorian house. The inn is well-placed for shopping at Kent's upscale stores, galleries, and chocolatier.

Governor Bradford Country House Inn

MAP F4 ▪ 250 Metacom Ave, Rte 136, Bristol, RI 02809 ▪ 401 254 9300 ▪ www.mounthopefarm. org ▪ $$

The 1745 grand mansion of historic landmark Mount Hope Farm allows you to feel like a true country squire.

The Griswold Inn

MAP D5 ▪ 36 Main St, Essex, CT 06426 ▪ 860 767 1776 ▪ www. griswoldinn.com ▪ $$

An Essex fixture since 1801, the "Gris" reflects the maritime history of this important port town. Five dining rooms dominate the historic structure, leaving guests to occupy the rooms at Hayden House next door. Breakfast costs extra.

Longfellow's Wayside Inn

MAP E2 ▪ 72 Wayside Inn Rd, Sudbury, MA 01776 ▪ 978 443 1776 ▪ www. wayside.org ▪ $$

The oldest operating inn in the US (since 1716), it was made famous by Longfellow's *Tales of a Wayside Inn*. The bar and dining rooms ooze antique charm.

Old Inn on the Green

MAP B3 ▪ 134 Hartsville-New Marlborough Rd, New Marlborough, MA 01230 ▪ 413 229 7924 ▪ www.oldinn.com ▪ $$

The spacious rooms of this circa-1800 inn, with

adjacent guesthouse on the picturesque village green, are decorated with country antiques, quilts, and folk art.

Red Lion Inn
MAP B3 ▪ 30 Main St, Stockbridge, MA 01262 ▪ 413 298 5545 ▪ www.redlioninn.com ▪ $$
The Red Lion has been welcoming travelers since just before the American Revolution, though the current main inn (there are several guest houses too) is a commodious Victorian structure with a perfect porch for sitting and rocking. The guest rooms are individually decorated and feature antiques. Breakfast is extra.

West Lane Inn
MAP B5 ▪ 22 West Lane, Ridgefield, CT 06877 ▪ 203 438 7323 ▪ www.westlaneinn.com ▪ $$
This spacious, gracious 1849 country inn sits on broad green lawns of a picture-perfect colonial town in southwestern Connecticut. A wrap-around porch invites indolent lazing, but many attractions are nearby. Includes free Wi-Fi and light breakfast. Fireplace rooms are available from October to March.

Country Inns (Northern)

Adair Country Inn
MAP L3 ▪ 80 Guider Lane, Bethlehem, NH 03574 ▪ 603 444 2600 ▪ www.adairinn.com ▪ $$
Each room in this romantic inn, which is located on a historic estate, is named after a nearby peak of the White Mountains. The setting

is perfect for watching wildlife and enjoying the alpine landscape.

Bethel Inn
MAP N3 ▪ 21 Broad St, Bethel, ME 04217 ▪ 207 824 2175 ▪ www.bethelinn.com ▪ $$
Bethel Inn is not far from Sunday River ski resort. The property includes a main inn (a cluster of four Colonial-style buildings), some townhouses, and a championship golf course. Rates include dinner, golf in summer, and cross-country trail fees in winter.

The Hancock Inn
MAP L6 ▪ 33 Main St, Hancock, NH 03449 ▪ 603 525 3318 ▪ www.hancockinn.com ▪ $$
This antique hostelry located in the Monadnock foothills has been operated continuously since 1789. The floorboards creak winsomely, but all rooms have modern facilities.

Inn at Shelburne Farms
MAP J3 ▪ 1611 Harbor Rd, Shelburne, VT 05482 ▪ 802 985 8498 ▪ www.shelburnefarms.org ▪ $$
This late 19th-century mansion overlooking Lake Champlain is the center-piece of a historic farm (see p111). The hotel's grounds were designed by Frederick Law Olmsted, known as the father of US landscape architecture.

Inn at Weston
MAP K5 ▪ 630 Main St, Rte 100, Weston, VT 05161 ▪ 802 824 6789 ▪ www.innweston.com ▪ $$
Dotted with orchids from the innkeeper's green-house, this romantic hideaway is concealed

in a charming village that is surrounded by ski mountains. It hosts small weddings and civil unions. Nine rooms boast fire-places, while some have double whirlpool tubs.

New London Inn
MAP L5 ▪ 353 Main St, New London, NH 03257 ▪ 603 526 2791 ▪ www.thenewlondoninn.com ▪ $$
This Federal-style 1792 inn has been transformed into a chic retreat with boldly artistic rooms. The owners wisely maintained the country-hotel look in all public areas, including the double-decker porch strewn with cozy wicker chairs and rockers.

Newcastle Inn
MAP P4 ▪ 60 River Rd, Newcastle, ME 04553 ▪ 207 563 5685 ▪ www.newcastleinn.com ▪ $$
Overlooking the Damariscotta River harbor, this country inn is perfectly situated for exploring the midcoast Maine peninsulas. Rooms are spread among main inn, cottage, and former carriage house; some have fireplaces. There's a guests-only pub, as well.

Quechee Inn at Marshland Farm
MAP K5 ▪ 1119 Quechee Main St, Quechee, VT 05059 ▪ 802 295 3133 ▪ www.quecheeinn.com ▪ $$
A spectacular setting across the road from the Quechee River makes this 1793 property a true country idyll. The rooms feel like spare bedrooms at grandma's house, but the comfortable rustic lounge features a welcoming fireplace.

Swift House Inn

MAP J4 ■ 25 Stewart Ln,
Middlebury, VT 05753
■ 802 388 9925 ■ www.
swifthouseinn.com ■ $$
The rooms are spread
across the Federal-era
main house, a modern-
ized carriage house, and a
small gatehouse set on a
hill above the picturesque
college town. Some rooms
benefit from fireplaces and
whirlpool tubs. Inclusive
breakfasts are generous.

Pitcher Inn

MAP K4 ■ 275 Main St,
Warren, VT 05674 ■ 802
496 6350 ■ www.pitcher
inn.com ■ $$$
Whimsical themed decor
in 11 rooms has won this
luxury property features
in practically every design
magazine. The Trout
Room has a bed of real
tree trunks, and a river-
stone fireplace.

Lakeside Lodgings

Hopkins Inn

MAP B4 ■ 22 Hopkins Rd,
New Preston, CT 06777
■ 860 868 7295 ■ www.
thehopkinsinn.com ■ $
A favorite escape for city
folks since 1847, this inn
standing on a knoll over-
looking the north shore of
Lake Waramaug adjoins
the Hopkins Vineyard.
Winter cross-country
skiing rivals the pleasures
of summer lakeside idling.

Inn at Smith Cove

MAP M5 ■ 19 Roberts Rd,
Gilford, NH 03249 ■ 603
293 1111 ■ www.innat
smithcove.com ■ $
This Victorian inn with
long, inviting porches and
a delightful gazebo on the
dock is located on a quiet,
charming corner of Lake
Winnipesaukee. The

quirky tower suite has a
bedroom, sitting room,
and whirlpool tub.

Inn on Newfound Lake

MAP L5 ■ 1030 Mayhew
Tpk, Rte 3A, Bridgewater,
NH 03222 ■ 603 744 9111
■ www.newfoundlake.
com ■ $$
This country stagecoach
inn on the Boston to
Montreal route has wel-
comed guests since 1840.
Renovation has created a
lavish Victorian showpiece.

Purity Spring Resort

MAP M4 ■ 1251 Eaton Rd,
Rte 153, East Madison,
NH 03849 ■ 603 367 8896
■ www.purityspring.com
■ $$
Loons aren't the only
repeat visitors to Purity
Lake; families come back
year after year to this
rustic resort founded in
the 19th century. In sum-
mer they paddle, in winter
they ski. Rates generally
include three meals daily.

Basin Harbor Club

MAP J4 ■ 4800 Basin
Harbor Rd, Vergennes, VT
05491 ■ 802 475 2311
■ www.basinharbor.com
■ $$$
Take one of 74 cabins or
book a room in the guest-
houses to join a resort
community at Basin
Harbor. Sailing and water-
skiing on Lake Champlain
(lessons are available) are
big summer hits. All meals
in summer are included.

Lodge at Moosehead Lake

MAP P1 ■ 368 Lily Bay Rd,
Greenville, ME 04441
■ 207 695 4400 ■ www.
lodgeatmooseheadlake.
com ■ $$$
Hand-carved beds and
spectacular views of

Maine's largest lake
enhance the modern
comforts on offer here.
Birding and moose-
watching add to the
wilderness experience. All
rooms are equipped with
a private bathroom, while
some also have a balcony.

Coastal Lodgings

Shore Acres

MAP J2 ■ 237 Shore Acres
Dr, North Hero Island, VT
■ 802 372 8722 ■ www.
shoreacres.com ■ $
Watch the sun rise
through morning mist on
Lake Champlain from one
of 19 lakeside rooms or
four garden-house rooms
a short walk away.

Atlantic Inn

MAP E6 ■ High St, Old
Harbor, Block Island ■ 401
466 5883 ■ late Apr–Oct
■ www.atlanticinn.com
■ $$
This 22-room Victorian
inn with an acclaimed
restaurant is just across
the street from Block
Island's best bathing
beach. The expansive
hillside property is dotted
with stunning gardens.

Atlantic Oceanside

MAP R3 ■ 119 Eden St,
Rte 3, Bar Harbor, ME
04609 ■ 207 288 5801
■ www.barharbormaine
hotel.com ■ $$
Set near the entrance
to Acadia National Park
(see pp14–15), the 12-acre
(4.5-ha) former estate of
Klondike billionaire Sir
Harry Oakes holds a
153-room resort with
jaw-dropping vistas of
Maine's rugged coast-
line. Guests also benefit
from indoor and outdoor
swimming pools and
a spa.

The Boathouse Waterfront Hotel
MAP N5 ▪ 21 Ocean Ave, Kennebunkport, ME 04046 ▪ 207 967 8223 ▪ www. boathousemе.com ▪ $$

Just steps from bustling Dock Square, this intimate waterfront hotel has 25 rooms, some with balconies looking out over the water, spread across two buildings. The rooms feature nautical elements, and have iPod docking stations and free Wi-Fi.

Cliff Lodge
MAP H5 ▪ 9 Cliff Rd, Nantucket, MA 02554 ▪ 508 228 9480 ▪ www. clifflodgenantucket.com ▪ $$

The 12 airy rooms in this 1771 whalemaster's eyrie above Nantucket Harbor embody a style that's half Old Nantucket, half Ralph Lauren. The inn's rooftop is a great vantage point for watching the sunset.

Edgartown Inn
MAP G5 ▪ 56 North Water St, Edgartown, Martha's Vineyard, MA 02539 ▪ 508 627 4794 ▪ Apr–Oct ▪ www.edgartowninn. com ▪ $$

With its white clapboards, cedar shingles, and large front porch, this 1798 sea captain's home is an iconic piece of Edgartown architecture. For greater seclusion, opt for a garden-house room.

Edgewater Motor Inn
MAP N5 ▪ 57 West Grand Ave, Old Orchard Beach, ME 04064 ▪ 207 934 2221 ▪ www.theedgewater motorinn.com ▪ $$

Five blocks west of the pier at Old Orchard Beach (see p126), this fabulously updated motel with a wide variety of rooms in different sizes stays open all year. No breakfast.

Inn at Castle Hill
MAP F2 ▪ 280 Argilla Rd, Ipswich, MA 01938 ▪ 978 412 2555 ▪ Apr–Dec ▪ www.theinnatcastlehill. com ▪ $$

Understated elegance and serenity characterize this tranquil inn on the Crane Estate. Walk to Crane Beach (see p52) backed by rolling sand dunes.

Island Inn
MAP Q4 ▪ Monhegan Island, ME 04852 ▪ 207 596 0371 ▪ late May–mid-Oct ▪ www.islandinn monhegan.com ▪ $$

This modernized 1816 inn above the ferry landing has some of the best views. Half the 32 rooms and suites have private baths but there's no TV or phones, and cellphone coverage is poor – which makes Monhegan more of a getaway than ever.

Steamboat Inn
MAP D5 ▪ 73 Steamboat Wharf, Mystic, CT 06355 ▪ 860 536 8300 ▪ www. steamboatinnmystic.com ▪ $$

With each room named for a vessel from Mystic's sailing heyday, this quirky riverside inn by the celebrated drawbridge is as nautical as it gets. Evening sherry and cookies are served.

Vineyard Harbor Motel
MAP G5 ▪ 60 Beach Rd, Vineyard Haven, MA 02568 ▪ 508 693 3334 ▪ www.vineyardharbor motel.com ▪ $$

The 40 rooms of this annually refreshed motel share a small private beach and every room has a refrigerator. Some even have full kitchens. It's on the island bus route and a 10-minute walk from the ferry dock.

Wellfleet Motel and Lodge
MAP H4 ▪ 170 Rte 6, South Wellfleet, MA 02663 ▪ 508 349 3535 ▪ late Apr–early Nov ▪ www. wellfleetmotel.com ▪ $$

Its location at the north end of the Cape Cod Rail Trail and across Rte 6 from the Audubon wildlife sanctuary is key, but so is the hospitality at this hybrid property of motel and lodge rooms. Many rooms have private patios or balconies overlooking a landscaped courtyard. Breakfast is included.

Camden Harbour Inn, Camden
MAP Q3 ▪ 83 Bayview St, Camden, ME 04843 ▪ 207 236 4200 ▪ www.camden harbourinn.com ▪ $$$

This romantic luxury boutique hotel pampers its guests with posh rooms, harbor views, wraparound porch, and Natalie's, one of the best fine-dining restaurants in Maine. Breakfast is extra.

Hyatt Regency Newport
MAP F5 ▪ 1 Goat Island, Newport, RI 02840 ▪ 401 851 1234 ▪ www.newport. hyatt.com ▪ $$$

Set on Goat Island in Narragansett Bay, this luxurious resort hotel is a quick boat ride from the Newport hubbub. The outdoor saltwater pool and long, green lawns are the perfect spot for lounging around.

Mountain Lodgings

Birch Ridge Inn

MAP K5 ▪ 37 Butler Rd, Killington, VT 05751 ▪ 802 422 4293 ▪ www. birchridge.com ▪ $

Located just a mile from Killington's slopes, this B&B has 10 contemporary guest rooms in a double A-frame lodge. Packages can cover lift tickets in winter and tee times in summer at nearby Killington Golf Resort. Popular for weddings.

Inn at Sunset Hill

MAP L3 ▪ 231 Sunset Hill Rd, Sugar Hill, NH ▪ 603 823 5522 ▪ www.innat sunsethill.com ▪ $

This country inn and adjacent farmhouse sit right outside Franconia Notch State Park. The inn offers a genteel base for winter activities in the White Mountains.

Mountain View Grand Resort & Spa

MAP L3 ▪ 101 Mountain View Rd, Whitefield, NH 03598 ▪ 866 484 3843 www.mountainviewgrand. com ▪ $$

This venerable hotel earns its name with stunning mountain views in two directions. It's perfect for both day hikers and alpine skiers.

Red Clover Inn

MAP K5 ▪ 7 Woodward Rd, Mendon, VT 05701 ▪ 802 775 2290 ▪ www. redcloverinn.com ▪ $$

This farm-based inn near Pico Peak is a well-kept secret among skiers. Rooms are cozy in the main inn, huge and comfy in the carriage-house. Breakfast is included.

Trapp Family Lodge

MAP K3 ▪ 700 Trapp Hill Rd, Stowe, VT 05672 ▪ 802 253 8511 ▪ www. trappfamily.com ▪ $$

This world-famous resort on the vast property of the family that inspired *The Sound of Music* has a large Austrian-style main lodge and 100 guesthouses. The cross-country ski trail is among the best in the US. Breakfast is extra.

Equinox Resort & Spa

MAP K6 ▪ 3567 Main St, Rte 7A, Manchester, VT 05254 ▪ 802 362 4700 ▪ www.equinoxresort. com ▪ $$$

Spacious, country-style rooms dot four buildings of this 18th-century resort with amazing mountain views. Outdoor activities on offer include boating, falconry, golf, fly-fishing, shooting, winter snowmobiling, and skiing.

Inn at Sawmill Farm

MAP K6 ▪ 7 Crosstown Rd, West Dover, VT 05356 ▪ 802 464 8131 ▪ www. theinnatsawmillfarm.com ▪ $$$

This winter-only inn is just up the road from the Mount Snow ski area, and the decor makes everything feel warm and cheery. The stylishly appointed rooms are generously sized for a historic inn. The Italian restaurant is superb.

Mountain Top Inn & Resort

MAP K4 ▪ 195 Mountain Top Rd, Chittendon VT 05737 ▪ 802 483 2311 ▪ www.mountaintopinn. com ▪ $$$

A true four-season resort with Nordic ski and snowshoe trails in winter, canoes and kayaks in summer. A choice of rustic-chic lodge rooms, cabins, or guesthouse make Mountain Top a splendid alpine getaway without the ski crowds.

Mount Washington Hotel & Resort

MAP M3 ▪ Rte 302, Bretton Woods, NH 03575 ▪ 603 278 1000 ▪ www. brettonwoods.com ▪ $$$

This palatial hotel offers upcountry elegance in a dramatic natural setting. In summer, golf is the main lure; in winter, it's skiing and dogsledding. The most popular package includes breakfast and dinner at any of the resort's five restaurants.

Stoweflake Mountain Resort & Spa

MAP K3 ▪ 1746 Mountain Rd, Stowe, VT 05672 ▪ 802 253 7355 ▪ www. stoweflake.com ▪ $$$

Set halfway up the access highway to the ski-and-hiking mecca of Mount Mansfield *(see p54)*, Stoweflake is the luxury choice in sports-crazed Stowe. Choose from gracious modern hotel or A-frame townhouses.

Woodstock Inn & Resort

MAP K5 ▪ 14 The Green, Woodstock, VT 05091 ▪ 802 457 1100 ▪ www. woodstockinn.com ▪ $$$

The Rockefellers built this huge modern pile to look as if it had been on the town green for centuries. Rooms have every conceivable comfort, but you'll find it hard to leave the lobby with its massive fieldstone fireplace.

Budget-Friendly Lodgings

Colonial Gables Oceanfront Village

MAP Q3 ■ 7 Eagle Lane, Belfast, ME 04915 ■ 207 338 4000 ■ May–Oct ■ www.colonialgables. com ■ $

Small cottages dot a hillside sloping down to a private beach on Penobscot Bay. Each of the cottages have their own kitchens and front porches. The property also has 13 motel rooms.

Curtis House Inn

MAP B5 ■ 506 Main St S, Woodbury, CT 06798 ■ 203 263 2101 ■ www. curtishouseinn.com ■ $

This mid-18th-century lodging retains its quirky style without the benefit of a designer makeover, even in upscale Woodbury. Some rooms are small or share baths.

Days Inn

MAP B3 ■ 372 Main St, Great Barrington, MA 01230 ■ 413 528 3150 ■ www.daysinn.com ■ $

This well-maintained chain motel with spacious rooms is right at the southern edge of town. It makes an excellent base for foraging for antiques in nearby South Egremont and Sheffield.

Herbert Grand Hotel

MAP N2 ■ 246 Main St, Kingfield, ME 04947 ■ 207 265 2000 ■ www.herbert grandhotel.com ■ $

Step back to 1918 at this marvelously old-fashioned mountain hotel close to Sugarloaf skiing and golf. The rooms are small, but all have baths.

The terrace over the portico serves as an evening social center.

The Inn at Long Trail

MAP K5 ■ 709 Rte 4, Sherburne Pass, Killington, VT 05751 ■ 802 775 7181 ■ www.innatlongtrail. com ■ $

Hikers adore this rustic lodge at the intersection of the Appalachian and Long trails in the heart of the Green Mountains. (There's a mail drop for through-hikers.) Vermont skiers also flock here. There's an Irish pub on site (see p112).

Kancamagus Swift River Inn

MAP M4 ■ 1316 Kancamagus Hwy, Albany, NH 03818 ■ 603 447 2332 ■ www. swiftriverinn.com ■ $

One of the rare lodgings on the Kancamagus Highway (see p60), this inn offers 10 spacious rooms with eclectic decor. North Conway shopping and White Mountain National Forest trails are nearby.

The Latchis Hotel & Theatre

MAP K6 ■ 50 Main St, Brattleboro, VT 05301 ■ 802 254 6300 ■ www. latchis.com ■ $

The Latchis is one of only two remaining Art Deco buildings in Vermont. It has modest rooms, free Wi-Fi, and a three-screen theater showing art and independent films.

Monhegan House

MAP Q4 ■ Main Rd, Mon-hegan Island, ME 04852 ■ 207 594 7983 ■ late May–early Oct ■ www. monheganhouse.com ■ $

Almost nothing has changed about this island

guesthouse since artists began flocking here to Monhegan Island (see p50) a century ago. The 28 rooms are over four floors, have beautiful views over the ocean, and are styled in "chic contemporary country" – but then they've always been that way.

Sandy Neck Motel

MAP G4 ■ 669 Rte 6A, Sandwich, MA 02537 ■ 508 362 3992 ■ Apr–Nov ■ www.sandyneck.com ■ $

This charming and well-kept older motel is sited at the entrance to the extensive sand bar of Sandy Neck Beach, near the tidal marshes famous for birding. No breakfast.

Breezeway Resort

MAP E5 ■ 70 Winnapaug Rd, Misquamicut, RI 02891 ■ 401 348 8953 ■ May–mid-Oct ■ www. breezewayresort.com ■ $$

Westerly's Misquamicut Beach (see p52) is a short walk from this family-friendly motel and apartment complex where every room has a refrigerator and some have cooking facilities. Guests can also make use of the outdoor pool and private beach area.

East Wind Inn

MAP Q4 ■ Mechanic St, Tenants Harbor, ME 04860 ■ 207 372 6366 ■ May–Oct ■ www.east windinn.com ■ $$

Wake to lobster boats heading out to haul their catch at this sprawling harborfront inn. Rooms are furnished with a mix of country furniture and local antiques. Some of the 26 rooms share baths.

Index

Acknowledgments

Author
Between them, Patricia Harris and David Lyon have experienced New England from the ground up, working such varied jobs as a commercial fisherman, travel tour leader, arts administrator, and restaurant line cook. They have lived in four New England states and traveled relentlessly in all six. In addition to co-authoring more than two dozen books, they write about travel, food, fine arts, and popular culture for magazines, newspapers, and websites, including HungryTravelers.com. They co-wrote DK's *Eyewitness Travel Guide to Boston* and *Top 10 Boston*.

Publishing Director Georgina Dee

Publisher Vivien Antwi

Design Director Phil Ormerod

Editorial Ankita Awasthi Tröger, Michelle Crane, Rachel Fox, Bharti Karakoti, Freddie Marriage, Alison McGill, Sally Schafer, Farah Sheikh, Jackie Staddon

Design Tessa Bindloss, Richard Czapnik, Marisa Renzullo

Commissioned Photography Alan Briere, David Lyons, Rough Guides/Dan Banniste, / Susannah Sayler, Tony Souter.

Picture Research Susie Peachey, Ellen Root, Lucy Sienkowska, Oran Tarjan.

Cartography Dominic Beddow, Subhashree Bharti, Simonetta Giori, James Macdonald

DTP Jason Little

Production Nancy-Jane Maun

Factchecker Patricia Harris, David Lyon

Proofreader Kathryn Glendenning

Indexer Hilary Bird

First edition created by Coppermill Books, London

Picture Credits
The publisher would like to thank the following for their kind permission to reproduce their photographs:
Key: a-above; b-below/bottom; c-centre; f-far; l-left; r-right; t-top

123RF.com: edella 96–7; Felix Lipov 107br; Juli Scalzi 86tl; sereznyi 97bl.

Abbe Museum: Ganessa Bryant 15clb. **Abbott's Lobster in the Rough:** 67tr. **Alamy Stock Photo:** age fotostock/Terrance Klassen 21br; Katharine Andriotis 101tr; Arcaid Images/Lucinda Lambton 28cl; Bill Bachmann 11cl; Norman Barrett 97cl; Vicki Beaver 76tl; David Brownell 31clb; Cal Sport Media/John Green 57tr; Chris Cameron 30–3l; Ken Clare 90cla; Thornton Cohen 19tl; Alan Copson 3tl, 74–5; Ian G Dagnall 4clb, 30bl, 33tl; Daniel Dempster Photography 37clb; DanitaDelimont.com/Cindy Miller Hopkins 64tr, /Walter Bibikow 17clb; Christian Delbert 58–9; Randy Duchaine 71cl,103bl, 130cla; EcoPhotography.com/Jerry and Marcy Monkman 27cr; Norman Eggert 11tr; Kevin Galvin 61tr; Granger; NYC. 36clb; Chase Guttman 124cl; hemis.fr / Philippe Renault 125br; Clarence Holmes Photography 14br; Andre Jenny 114tl; Mark Klein 117cl; David Litschel 129cra; David Lyons 27tl; Terry Mathews 57cl; Henk Meijer 2tl, 8–9; Mira 1, 3tr, 18br, 115b, 132–3; MiraMira 18–19, 109tl; Nikreates 13tc; noblelMAGES/David Noble 4crb, 51cl; George Ostertag 56br; Pat & Chuck Blackley 53cr; Susan Pease 108clb; Major Pix 88tl; George Robinson 71br; Pierre Rochon 131bl; Stephen Saks Photography 68tl; Kumar Sriskandan 49b; Stan Tess 53bl, 63tr, 73tr; Steve Tulley 2tr, 34–5; Frank Vetere 31tl; Freddy Boom Boom Washington 21tl; ZUMApress.comSouthcreek Global/Geoff Bolte 71tr. **AWL Images:** Demetrio Carrasco 4cl; Danita Delimont Stock 22–3, 61br.

Banyan Bar + Refuge: 83b. **Barbara Lynch Gruppo:** Brian Samuels 82tr; WEC Photos 66cl. **Boston Symphony Orchestra:** Hilary Scot 33br.

Cabot Creamery: 111br. **Cape Neddick Lobster Pound:** 128crb. **Castle Street Café:** 85clb. **Center for Historic Shipwreck Preservation:** Kenneth Garrett 47c. **The Clam Shack:** Daryl Getman 128ca. **Craigie On Main:** 66tr.

Discover New England: Connecticut Office of Tourism /Kindra Clineff 96tl, 99crb, /Robert Gregson 95tl; Maine Office of Tourism 104–5, 122cla, /Steve Bly 123cr; New Hampshire Division of Travel and Tourism Development 115tr; Phil Savignano 124t; Vermont Department of Tourism & Marketing 106tr, 107t; Yale University Art Gallery/Michael Marsland 95crb. **Dreamstime.com:** Alpegor 10cl; Allwoodphoto 51tr; Americanspirit 94tl; Xavier Ascanio 60cra; Jon Bilous 4t,12–13, 20clb, 20–21, 52t; Paul Brady 88br; Chrissierackl 11bl,116t; Angel Claudio 16–17; Cllhnstev 48bl; Ken Cole 14–15; Jerry Coli 4b, 92bl; Christian Delbert 28–9; Songquan Deng 11cra; Eric Broder Van Dyke 29tl; Fashionstock.com 11cla; Stephen Gass 80b; Vlad Ghiea 15tl; Pierrette Guertin 79cl; Jeffrey Holcombe 24–5; Wangkun Jia 28br,108br, 116bl, 123t; Brian Kushner 25tl; Chee-onn Leong 126b; Daniel Logan 87cr; Maglara 77tl; Giuseppe Di Paolo 78b; Sean Pavone 87t; Peanutroaster 118bl; Rolf52 77crb; Jorge Salcedo 10cla; Lee Snider 25bl, 26bc, 48tr; Suchan 38b; Vividrange 12br; Colin Young 32cla.

Farnsworth Art Museum: Gift of Mr. and Mrs. Charles Shipman Payson *Romance of Autumn* (1916) George Bellows Oil on canvas 41¾ x 49⅝ inches, 1964.1366 45cl. **Freedom Trail Foundation:** 70c. **Frosty Drew Nature Center & Observatory:** 89cl.

Getty Images: AFP/Cesar Rangel 45tr; Bloomberg/Herb Swanson 65tr; Boynlarge/Carol M. Highsmith 50–51; GraphicaArtis 36tr; Brian D. Kersey 69tr; Jack Mitchell 41tr; Portland Press Herald/John Ewing 127cra; Ron Thomas 26–7; Barry Winiker 17cr. **Green Mountain Club:** Jocelyn Hebert 56tl. **Green River Festival:** Flora Reed 73cl. **Greenwich Historical Society:** 98cla.

Harbour House: Tom Bombria 100b. **Harvard Art Museums:** 42tc. **The Hawthorne:** Gustav Holland 82cl.

Isabella Stewart Gardner Museum: Nic Lehoux .0tl.

John F. Kennedy Library Foundation: 44cla. courtesy of **Lake Champlain Chocolates:** 111ca. **Max Restaurant Group:** Photo Credit: LibbyVision. com 102tl. **Montshire Museum:** 110tl. **The Mount, Lenox, MA:** John Seakwood 44br. **Photograph ©** 2011 Museum of Fine Arts, Boston: 40br. **Mystic Seaport, Mystic, CT:** 46b.

courtesy of the **Nantucket Historical Association:** Peter Vanderwarker 46tl. **National Parks Service:** 4cr. **NECI on Main:** Brett Simison 13cr. **New England Aquarium:** Webb Chappell 53cl. **Newport Jazz Festival:** Douglas Mason 72b. **Photo courtesy of Norman Rockwell Museum, Stockbridge, Massachusetts:** 32clb.

Ocean House: 91b. **Omni Mount Washington Resort:** 54b.

Perfect Wife: 112clb. **Peter Pots Pottery:** 93c. **Pilgrim Hall Museum:** 78ca. **Prohibition Pig:** Prohibition Pig 112ca.

Ramblewild: 62tl. **Rex by Shutterstock:** Stock Connection 10br; ZUMA Wire/Ricky Bassman 37tr. **Courtesy of the RISD Museum:** 93tl, Bequest of Mrs. Edith Stuyvesant Vanderbilt Gerry *Le Repos* (Repose) (ca. 1870–1871) Édouard Manet 43tl. **Robert Harding Picture Library:** Alan Copson 60clb; Robert Francis 18clb. **Roger Williams Park Zoo:** 62br.

Sandwich Glass Museum: 84ca. **Shelburne Farms:** Vera Chang 66br. **Sledventures:** 119cr. **Sugarloaf Mountain:** Jamie Walter 55cla. **Sunday River Resort:** Shelley Bowen 4cla; Dave Pecunies 54tl. **SuperStock:** age fotostock/Jannis Werner 13cr; /John Greim 11crb, 16ca, /Nikhilesh Haval 7cr; Food and Drink/Tim Hill 65cl; imageBROKER 10cb; Travel Library Limited 24clb.

Wadsworth Atheneum: 41cl. **Williamstown Theatre Festival:** T Charles Erickson Photography 81cla. **Woodstock Inn, Station & Brewery:** John W. Hession 120crb. **Wright Museum of World War II:** 118ca.

Yale University Art Gallery: Elizabeth Felicella 70bl; Michael Marsland 42bl.

Cover
Front and spine: **Alamy Stock Photo:** David Brownell
Back: **Dreamstime.com:** Bleukrabbe.

Pull Out Map Cover
Alamy Stock Photo: David Brownell.

All other images © Dorling Kindersley
For further information see: www.dkimages.com

As a guide to abbreviations in visitor information blocks: **Adm** = admission charge; **B** = breakfast; **D** = dinner; **L** = lunch.

Printed and bound in China

First American edition, 2010
Published in the United States by
DK Publishing, 345 Hudson Street,
New York, New York 10014

Copyright 2010, 2017 © Dorling Kindersley Limited

A Penguin Random House Company

17 18 19 20 10 9 8 7 6 5 4 3 2

Reprinted with revisions 2012, 2014, 2017

All rights reserved. Without limiting the rights under the copyright reserved above, no part of this publication may be reproduced, stored in or introduced into a retrieval system, or transmitted, in any form, or by any means (electronic, mechanical, photocopying, recording, or otherwise), without the prior written permission of the copyright owner.

Published in the UK by Dorling Kindersley Limited.

A catalog record for this book is available from the Library of Congress.

ISSN 1479-344X
ISBN 978 1 4654 6021 9

New England: Selected Index of Places